The Ancient Black Civilizations of Asia

By

Dr. Clyde Winters

Table of Contents

Introduction

The Ancient Black Civilizations of Asia , is richly illustrated. These pictures come from a wonderful history site called: The World's First Civilizations were All Black Civilizations http://www.realhistorywww.com .

Since the Atlantic slave trade a myth has become fact that African/Black people did not have any civilization. This myth was created to justify the enslavement of Africans in the Americas.

In The Ancient Black Civilizations of Asia , we will examine and discuss the linguistic, anthropological, historical evidence supporting the origination of civilization in Asia by Blacks from Africa, known in history as the Kushites.

There is constant discussion about Eurocentric and Afrocentric history. In this book we will discuss the history of Black/African civilizations in ancient Asia.

Blacks writing ancient history have always been discouraged.

They tell African people to write about slavery and the African

kingdoms, everything else should be written by Europeans.

African researchers should not limit themselves to these periods of history writing. We must write about ancient history because this situates a people in time and culture. In the U.S., there are constant demands for Universities to return to teaching the Classics from Greece and Rome. Yet many Black people at University do not even study their history because they feel that all they need is to be credentialed in some field so they can get a job.

Knowing your history will reinvigorate your mind and spirit. Amos Wilson in <u>The Falsification of Afrikan consciousness:</u> <u>Eurocentric history, psychiatry and the politics of white</u> <u>supremacy</u> believes that the African spirit and mind can be healed through the advancement of African centered historiagraphic, social and natural sciences. Wilson wrote "Apparently the rewriting, the distortion and the stealing of our history must serve vital economic, political and social functions for the Europeans or else he would not bother and try so hard to keep our history away from us, and to distort it in our own minds" (p.15).

To Wilson we should see history as psychohistory, since the aim of writing Black people out of history is to destroy any sense of intellectual or social self-esteem for African people. Wilson noted that" In the final analysis, European history's principal function is to first separate us from ourselves and separate us from the reality of the world; to separate us from the reality of our history and to separate us from its ramifications"(p.24).

Dr. Wilson maintains that we must study Afrocentric History, because Europeans use history as a way of maintaining white supremacy; and the study of history by Blacks is a threat to the status quo.

Most people belief that the writing of history is neutral. Writing history is not neutral. Michael Parenti, in History as Mystery (1999), believes that history is not neutral. In his opinion history is written by the ruling class to solidify their position. He observed that "much written history is an ideologically safe commodity. It might best be called "mainstream history", "orthodox history", "conventional history" and even "ruling-class history" because it presents the dominant perspective of the affluent people who preside over the major institutions of society" (p.xi).

Parenti, supports Wilsons' view on the impact of Eurocentrism on education when he noted that " many history and political science programs offered in middle and higher education rest on a Eurocentric bias" (p.xiv). As a result, Parenti argues that we

learned a "disinformational history" which represents the views of the ruling class rather than real history (p.10). As a result, Parenti claims that we have "consensus history textbooks" that teaches history from a distorted base.

The comments of Wilson and Parenti make it clear that history is not written from a neutral perspective, it is written by historians who define what history is or is not. This means that due to dozal, the personality and preconceptions of the historians determine how he writes history. As a result, we find that "establishment" historians usually write history which supports the dominant view of the ruling class, which primarily support institutions of higher learning through well funded endowments.

The allegiance of a particular historian to a class or "association"

means that when the historian identifies, selects and interprets

facts, and the framework used to appraise the facts will be guided

the truths accepted by the "association" or social class. This is

why Jacques Berlinerblau, in Heresy in the University: The Black

Athena controversy and the responsibilities of American

intellectuals (1999), observed that "How can a social-scientist, a

historian, a literary criticism etc., claim that his or her conclusion

are in any way true when it is so abundantly clear that these

conclusions are inextricably bound with the social and political

contexts in which he or she works and lives?"(p.192).

Since history is written from the perspective of the person

writing history, an Afrocentric scholar's work should be respect ᴇᴄ(

just as much as the writing of a Eurocentric or "establishment"

historian, but this is not the case.

This is why both Eurocentric and so-called Liberal historians

will usually agree that Blacks lack any type of ancient history, or association with Egyptian history. They agree, because both groups do not believe that Blacks have a ancient history due to their absorption of "consensus history", that deny any role of blacks in ancient history except as "Ethiopian" or "Nubian" slaves among the Greeks, Romans and Egyptians.

We assume that any article or book written by an establishment member of the academe is best on valid historical truths, erudite scholarship and impeccable research. Although insiders and outsiders alike, sociological research indicates that there are unconscious cognitive structures within each individual hold this view idealistic view of members of the academe that determine how they perceive "reality". These structures are called doxa.

Commenting on these schema Berlinerblau noted that "These types of theories share the assumption that human beings know things that they do not even know that they know; that they "possess" knowledge about the world which exists in some sort of cognitive substrate, beyond the realm of discourse" (p.106).

Wacquant says that doxa is " a realm of implicit and unstated beliefs".

Given the research suggesting that doxa exist, support the view that some researchers allow their hatred of multiculturalism to define their discourse on teaching and writing by Afrocentrists and multiculturalists. Moreover, it suggests that when topics such as Afrocentrism are attacked by members of the academe, these academics are supported by the "establishment" without any reservation or test of the validity of their claims. In fact, it appears that doxic assumptions relating to the invalidity of Afrocentrism obviates critique of the academics that disparage Afrocentrist research. This research is attacked by these scholars without the scholars presenting any counter evidence to falsify the Afrocentric position.

People in Afrocentric studies are serious scholars. They use the same methods that other scientists use, the only difference is that they look at issues from an africalogical perspective. There is nothing wrong in taking such a perspective since all history is written from the personal perspective of the historian writing that history. If your frame of reference for Afrocentric study is based solely on the views of outsiders: Liberals and Eurocentrists you will spend the rest of your life trying to prove that Black people have a history, when Eurocentric and liberal European researchers already know that **WE HAVE A HISTORY**.

Finally we can see the real problem Euronuts have with Afrocentrism,. The problem is Afrocentrism is a reminder of the true historical experiences that make up world history.

If we make you feel you don't have a history that is not our problem. It may be a product of an inferiority complex developed among non-Mediterranean Europeans who know they have no history.

Afro-Americans (AAs), like W.E.B. DuBois were the first Blacks to write history. These Blacks studied Greek and Latin. They read the Greeco-Roman literature and discovered that the Greeco-Romans did not mind admitting that 1) the Egyptians were Black,2) the Kushites founded civilization in Africa and Eurasia ;

and 3) the first inhabitants of Greece and Rome were Blacks from Africa. These three facts are the ancient **Model of History**.

It is the Greeco-Roman literature that state 1) the Egyptians were Black, 2) the Kushites founded civilization in Africa and Eurasia ; and 3) the first inhabitants of Greece and Rome were Blacks from Africa. This means that when Afrocentric scholars confirm aspects of the Ancient Model of history they are not showing racism toward whites, they are acknowleding historical realities first chronicled by white Greeks and Romans.

To claim the Afrocentric researchers seek to dehunanize whites, based on historical facts first developed and elaborated by white Greeks and Romans is laughable.It is people like you who are the haters--since the foundation of your anger shoul be directed at the white Greeks and Romans--not Afrocentric researchers who originally began their research based on Greeco-Roman literature. Afro-American scholars can't help the fact that the Ancient Model of history was later confirmed by archaeology, crianiometrics and the decipherment of ancient text. Look in the mirror and see the truth.

If Greeco-Roman literature, archaeology, ancient text and crianiometrics (science you invented) make you feel the Ancient Model of history "[seeks] to demean & dehumanize us [whites] by stealing our history, our heritage, our very identities.[And] That you seek to do us harm by getting us to think we have no history, no heritage, no identities, & no homeland to call our own." Is a product of delusional thinking, since it was the Greeco-Romans who created the ancient model of history.

Afrocentric researchers should not be blamed for your inferiority complex. Your inferiority complex is the product of being taught lies by Western European scholars especially the Germans.

The Germans and Britains created the myth that European history was began with the Greeks and Romans. They also invented the lie that Egyptians and other founders of the River Valley civilizations were Black skinned 'whites'.

You accepted the lie that founders of the River Valley
civilization were Black skinned whites until you looked in the
mirror--and saw you looked nothing like these people who you
recognized looked like the AAs who live among you.

Recognition that the Black skinned 'whites' looked exactly like
the AAs you hate but envy, made you feel even more inferior.
You were able to keep down your fury until you read Afrocentric
text which expanded the Ancient Model of history by confirming
this history using the results of archaeological, linguistic and
craniometric research.

Euronuts hate Afrocentrism because it uses social sciences:
history, linguistics, archaeology and genetics to further confirm
the Ancient Model of history and then publish them in journals.

Afrocentric researchers are hated because they have created
beautiful websites that spread the truth, and provides wonderful
pages full of visual evidence documenting the truths that come
from knowing the Ancient Model of history given us by the
Greeco-Romans.

If you feel Afrocentrism "[seeks] to demean & dehumanize us [whites] by stealing our history, our heritage, our very identities.[And] That you seek to do us harm by getting us to think we have no history, no heritage, no identities, & no homeland to call our own", blame these emotions on the Greeco-Romans and the history lies taught you by your teachers--not Afrocentric researchers.

Afrocentric researchers do not hate whites. If what we write disturbs you that is your problem based on the lies you have accepted as a result of your schooling. You may find peace if you accept the Ancient Model of history, which has nothing to do with Afrocentrism. it is a Model of History absent the history lies taught you by your teachers.

Chapter 1 : Arabia

The earliest civilization in Southwest Arabia date back to the 2nd Millenium. This culture is called the Tihama culture which originated in Africa[1] .

This view is supported by the archaeological evidence that support a close relationship between the Puntites/ Ethiopians and Nubians. For example, according to Fattovich, the pottery from Tihama Cultural Complex and other Ethiopian sites shows similarities to the Kerma and C-Group pottery[2]. Given this connection between Ethiopian civilizations and civilizations in Nubia, make it clear that the Ethiopians would have been familiar with the ancient writing system used in this area.

---

[1] Rudolfo Fattovich, The development of urbanism in the Northern Horn of Africa in ancient and Medieval Times. Retrieved 2/19/2008
http://www.arkeologi.uu.se/afr/projects/BOOK/fattowich.pdf
[22] Ibid., passim .

At Tihama and other sites in Arabia we find pottery related to the

C-Group people of Nubia [3].The archaeological evidence indicates

that C-Group people expanded from Nubia to Mesopotamia and

the Indus Valley.

The Tihama civilization originated in Nubia. It is characterized

by the cheesecake or pillbox burial monuments which extend

from Dhofar in Nubia, the Gara mountains to Adulis on the Gulf of

Zula, to Hadramaut, Qataban, Ausan, Adenm, Asir, the Main area

and Tihama.

The historical evidence support an old presence of Ethio-Semitic

in Africa. For example, the Axumite Empire was founded by the

Habashan. the habashan are mentioned in a 3rd or 4th century

---

[3] Keall, E. J. (2000), Changing Settlement along the Red Sea Coast of Yemen in the Bronze Age=, First International Congress on the Archaeology of the Ancient Near East (Rome May 18-23, 1998), Proceedings, (Matthiae, P., Enea, A., Peyronel, L. and Pinnock, F., eds), 719-31, Rome; Giumlia-Mair, A., Keall, E. J., Shugar, A. and Stock, S. (2002) ,Investigation of a Copper-based Hoard from the Megalithic Site of al-Midamman, Yemen: an Interdisciplinary Approach, Journal of Archaeological Science 29, 195-209; and E.J. Keall, Dr.J. Edward , Contact across the Red Sea (between Arabia and Africa) in the 2nd millennium BC: circumstantial evidence from the archaeological site of al-Midamman, Tihama coast of Yemen, and Dahlak Kabir Island, Eritrea .

Himyarite inscription from South Arabia, which refers to an alliance between Gadarat King of the Habashan or Habashat.

Some of the people of Punt were probably Tigrinya speakers, who call their language habesha, i.e., Abyssinian par excellence. The term Habesh, seems to represent an old name for Abyssinia and may be connected with the Amharic word **washa** 'cave or cavern', and may refer to the" cave dwellers" who once served as the principal traders along the Ethiopian coast. The ability of the Ethiopians as sailors, is supported by the title bahr nagash, "ruler of the maritime province" or Eritrea.

In addition, some of the earliest Sabean/Thamudic inscriptions have been found in Ethiopia, and not South Arabia. For example, Dr. Doresse has found Sabean cursive writing on a sceptre that indicates that the Habashat/Axumite empire had writing.

These Habashan are mentioned in Egyptian inscriptions of the 18th Dynasty (1709-1320) in connection to the land of Punt. Given the Egyptian association of the Habashan with Punt, I call the speakers of the Ethio-Semitic languages: Puntites. We have Egyptian evidence of trade missions to Punt as early as PepiII in 2400 BC and Mentuholep IV and IV. The vizier Amenemhat, of Mentuholep IV is said to have established a port near Safaga. the most famous mission to Punt was sent by Queen Hatshepsut, and is recorded at deir el Bahri. Since the Habashan are mentioned in Egyptian documents they were in existence long before the Arabic speakers.

The evidence of shared archaism for Akkadian and Ethio-Semitic indicate that the speakers of these languages probably shared many linguistic features when they separated. It also suggest that thespeakers of these languages probably separated in Africa, since the Ethio-Semitic speakers have long been established in their present home, as supported by the Egyptian inscriptions. The Ethio-Semitic speakers have maintained these features due to the relative stability of these languages[4]. We must conclude that the Semitic languages originated in Africa.

---

[4] Clyde Winters, Linguistic Continuity and African and Dravidian languages", International Journal of Dravidian Linguistics, 23 (2), (1996) 34-52.

The ancient Arabians were called Adites. The Adites had come from ancient northeast Africa. The whole of Arabia was ruled by these Blacks until the Ninth century BC when Jectanid or white tribes defeated the northern Adite kingdoms. This marked the first large influx of whites into Arabia. It was from this and later invasion of Indo-European people which led to the present mix-race group we call Arabs today.

Even after the Indo-Europeans destroyed most of Arabia's ancient civilization, civilization remained in South Arabia. The South Arabian cultures were of Ethiopean origin. This culture dates to 1100 BC.

The Arabia civilizations were mainly city-states. The include Saba, with its capital at Marib; Qatabam, with its capital at Timna; Hadhramut with its capital at Shabwa; Ma'in with its capital at Qarnaw; and Ansan which was located between Qataban and Hadhramut. The traders of these cities traded with people in Bagdad, Alexandria and Damascus.

The rulers of these cities were called "*Mukkaribs*". The title "Mukkarib" probably meant "priest-king".

The South Arabians lived in peace. There were few wars between the South Arabian cities.

The South Arabians used irrigation to grow crops. Dams were built to deflect the runoff from occasional rain onto irrigation canal. They also dug wells to provide water for the fields. They made beautiful temples and art work.

The South Arabian civilization was destroyed by Jectanide tribes.

In A.D. 50 , under a new line of kings Axum became the leading nation on the Red Sea. Due to Axumite power they controlled the key harbors on both sides of the Red Sea. Prof. Godbey, says that tradition has it that every since King Menelik I, took the throne, the Abyssinia Kings who lived on both sides of the Red Sea (Yemen and Abyssinia) were known as "**Bar Nagash**" or"Sea Kings". The Himyarite kings after 250 BC, controlled many of the ports on both sides of the Red Sea.

In an inscription written in Ethiopic Ezana , king of Axum proclaimed that he had conquered Meroe and a huge empire including the South Arabian states of Himyar, Haidan, and Saba.

In the 6th century A.D. rebelliousness Axumite troops established an independent kingdom in Yemen and the Abyssinians gained greater control of South Arabia. By the 7th century A.D., the Persians had taken control of the Yemenite ports and the Axumites were driven out of South Arabia.

The Axumites because of their total control of the South Arabia from the 1st to the 3rd centuries A.D. held sway over much of the Indian Ocean trade.In addition up until the 5th century A.D. the Abyssinians controlled the caravan routes of Southern Arabia. Moreover, because of the Persian use of former Axumite officials to administer Yemen, the Abyssinia continued to have influence even after they lost political control of the region.

Chapter 2: The Kushite Spread from Africa to Eurasia

Archaeogenetics is the use of genetics, archaeology and linguistics to explain and discuss the origin and spread of homo sapien sapiens[5]. In this paper we will use archaeogenetics to examine and discuss the spread of haplogroup R-M173 by the ancient Kushites.

Researchers have outlined two possible out of Africa events in the past 40ky. Although these out of Africa events occurred during prehistory the Classical writers of Greece and Rome discussed a recent migration of people from Africa into Eurasia. This African population was called: Kushites.

The Kushites originated in the Highland Regions of Africa 8kya. They were the ancestors of the Niger-Congo speakers[6] .

---

[5]Renfrew, C. 2010. Archaeogenetics—Towards a 'New Synthesis'? *Cur Biol*, (February 23, 2010) 20:R162-R165.

[6] Winters C. Origin of the Niger-Congo Speakers. WebmedCentral GENETICS 2012;3(3):WMC003149 http://www.webmedcentral.com/article_view/3149

A review of the archaeological, linguistic, genomic and craniometric literature was used to explore the role of the Kushites in the spread of haplogroup R from Africa to Eurasia. In this analysis of the linguistic, craniometric, and related scientific literatures we will determine if archaeological and genomic evidence can trace a migration event and dispersal of Kushites into Eurasia as maintained by the Classical writers.

I analyzed the craniometric , linguistic, archaeological and y-chromosome sequences of African and Eurasian populations from the literature relating to these diverse fields.

This literature provides us with a critical examination of the distribution of R1*-M173 . It presents a genetic pattern of this haplogroup from Africa to Eurasia, and the dispersal of a significant African male contribution to Eurasia in the past 4ky.

The pristine form of R1*M173 is found only in Africa (Cruciani et al, 2002, 2010). Haplogroup R1*-M173 (xSRY 10831, M18, M117, M173,M269). Haplogroup R-M173 is ancestral to R-P25 (xM269) and other Eurasian downstream markers.

The Eurasian R1b y-chromosome has the M269 mutation. The R-P25* haplogroup has been found in Europe, West and East Asia .

Figure 1 we see the frequency of R1*-M173 in Africa and Eurasia. InThe frequency of Y-chromosome R1*-M173 in Africa range between 7-95% and averages 39.5% . The R*-M173 (haplotype 117) chromosome is found frequently in Africa, but rare to extremely low frequencies in Eurasia. The Eurasian R haplogroup is characterized by R1b3-M269. The M269 derived allele has a M207/M173 background.

In Figure 1 we provide the frequencies of y-chromosome M-173 in Africa and Eurasia. Whereas only between 8% and 10% of M-173 is carried by Eurasians, 82% of the carriers of this y-chromosome are found in Africa.

Coia et al provides substantial data that the presence of R1*-M173 did not follow the spread of the spread of mtDNA haplogroup U6 in Sub-Saharan Africa, which is found in North Africa . This suggest that R1*-M173 may not be the result of back migration from Asia if this theory depends on the spread of

haplogroup U6 in areas where R1*-M173 is found.

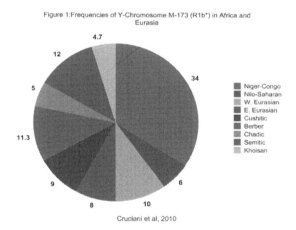

Figure 1:Frequencies of Y-Chromosome M-173 (R1b*) in Africa and Eurasia

Cruciani et al, 2010

The majority of West Africans formerly lived just below Egypt in

Nubia, before they moved westward into Cameroon, the Niger

Valley and Senegambian regions. This part of Africa was inhabited by the Kushite people in ancient times.

According to Underhill the geographical origin of y-chromosome R1b is situated in Eurasia. As a result, these researchers believed that the R y-chromosome haplogroup in Africa suggest a back migration from Asia to Africa [7].

Cruciani et al , assume that the phylogeographic y-haplotype analyses suggest that Asia was probably the home for y-chromosome M173 and that the presence of haplotype M173 is due to a back migration from Asia since haplogroup R chromosomes were found in Cameroon [8]. Although this was Cruciani et al , opinion the phylogeography, diversity and widespread nature of M173 across the African continent implies that haplotype M173 probably originated in Africa, and that it expanded into Asia recently.

---

[7] Cruciani,F., Trombetta,B., Sellitto, D., Massaia,A. destroy-Bisol,G., Watson, E., Colomb, E.B. (2010) Eur J. Hum Genet.,(6 January 2010) doi:10.1038/ejhg.2009.231: 1-8.

[8] Cruciani, F., Santolamazza,P., Shen, P., Macaulay, V., Moral P., Olckers,A. (2002) A Back Migration from Asia to Sub-Saharan Africa is supported by High-Resolution Analysis of Human Y-chromosome Haplotypes. Am J. Hum Genet., 70,1197-1214.

The aggregated African populations with an R-M173 DNA profile were disaggregated to determine the distribution of R-M173 in Sub-Saharan Africa. I analyzed the y-chromosome sequences of the R haplogroup from Africa and Asia. This review of prior literature on macrohaplogroup R allowed us to critically look at the distribution of R lineages across the African continent.

The greatest diversity of haplogroup R is found in Africa not Asia [9] . The distribution of haplogroup R in Africa increases moving from east to west [10].

The Eurasian form of haplogroup R, include R1a (SRY1532) and R1b (M269). Haplogroup R1-M173 is ancestral to R-P25 (xM269) and other Eurasian downstream lineages.

In Asia the frequency of haplotype M173 is as follows: Anatolia 0.19%, Iran 2.67%, Iraq 0.49% Oman 1.0%, Pakistan 0.57% and Oman 1.0% . This contrast sharply with the widespread

[9] Clyde Winters, Possible African Origin of R-M173.

[10] Clyde Winters (2010). The Kushite Spread of Haplogroup R1*-M173 from Africa to Eurasia. Current Research Journal of Biological Sciences 2(4): 294-299. http://maxwellsci.com/print/crjbs/v2-294-299.pdf

distribution of R1*-M173 in Africa, that ranges between 7-95% and averages 39% ; but no trace of Eurasiatic maternal lineages in West Central Africa.

Y-chromosome R1 is found throghout Africa. The pristine form of R1-M173 is only found in Africa [11]. The age of y-chromosome R is 27ky. Most researchers believe that R(M173) is 18.5 ky.

There is a great diversity of the macrohaplogroup R in Africa . Y-chromosome R is characterized by M207/V45. The V45 mutation is found among African populations [12]. ISOGG 2010 Y-DNA haplogroup tree makes it clear that V45 is phylogenetically equivalent to M207.

[11]Coia, V. , Destro-Bisol,G., Verginelli F., Battaggia,C., Boschi,I.,, Cruciani,F.,Spedini,G., Comas,D., and Calafell,F. (2005) Brief communication: mtDNA variation in North Cameroon: lack of Asian lineages and implications for back migration from Asia to sub-Saharan Africa, Am J Phys Anthropol (http://www3.interscience.wiley.com/cgi-bin/fulltext/110495269/PDFSTART) (electronically published May 13, 2005; accessed August 5, 2005).

[12]Cruciani et al, 2010

The most common R haplogroup in Africa is R1 (M173). The predominant haplogroup is R1b [13]. Cruciani et al discovered new R1b mutations including V7, V8, V45, V69, and V88.

Geography appears to play a significant role in the distribution of haplogroup R in Africa. Cruciani has renamed the R*-M173 (R P-25) in Africa V88. The TMRCA of V88 was 9200-5600 kya .

Y-chromosome V88 (R1b1a) has its highest frequency among Chadic speakers, while the carriers of V88 among Niger-Congo speakers (predominately Bantu people) range between 2-66% [14] . Haplogroup V88 includes the mutations M18, V35 and V7. Cruciani et al revealed that R-V88 is also carried by Eurasians including the distinctive mutations M18, V35 and V7.

R1b1-P25 is found in Western Eurasia. Haplogroup R1b1* is found in Africa at various frequencies. Berniell-Lee et al found in their study that 5.2% carried Rb1*. The frequency of R1b1*

[13]Winters, C.(2010b)Letter: The Fulani are not from the Middle East. PNAS.
http://www.pnas.org/content/107/34/E132.full

[14] Berniell-Lee, G., Calafell, F., Bosch ,E. ,Heyer, E, Sica, L., Mouguiama-Daouda,¹ P., van der Veen, L., Hombert, J-M., Quintana-Murci , L.and, Comas, D. (2009) Genetic and Demographic Implications of the Bantu Expansion: Insights from Human Paternal Lineages, Mol. Bio. and Evol. 26(7),1581-1589; doi:10.1093/molbev/msp069.

among the Bantu ranged from 2-20. The bearers of R1b1* among the Pygmy populations ranged from 1-25% . The frequency of R1b1 among Guinea-Bissau populations was 12%[15] .

Most Eurasians carry the M269 (R1b1b2) mutation. The subclades of R1b1b2 include Rh1b1b2g (U106) (TMRCA 8.3kya) and R1b1b2h (U152) (TMRCA 7.4kya)

The most recent common ancestor for R1b1b2 in Europe is probably 8kya [16]. Y-Chromosome R1b1b2 has high frequencies in England, France, Italy and Germany .

Around 0.1 of Sub Saharan Africans carry R1b1b2. Wood et al found that Khoisan (2.2%) and Niger-Congo (0.4%) speakers carried the R-M269 y-chromosome[17].

---

[15] Carvalho M, Brito P, Bento AM, Gomes V, Antunes H, Costa HA, Lopes V, Serra A, Balsa F, Andrade L, Anjos MJ, Corte-Real F, Gusmão L. (2011).Paternal and maternal lineages in Guinea-Bissau population. Forensic Sci Int Genet. 5(2),114-6.

[16] Balaresque, P., Bowden, G.R., Adams, S.M., Leung, H-Y, King, T.E., et al. (2010) A Predominantly Neolithic Origin for European Paternal Lineages. PLoS Biol 8(1): e1000285.doi:10.1371/journal.pbio.1000285
http://www.plosbiology.org/article/info%3Adoi%2F10.1371%2Fjournal.pbio.100002 85

[17] Wood,E.T., Stover,D.A., Ehret,C., Destro-Bisol,G., Spedini,G., McLeod, H., Louie,L., Bamshad,M., Strassmann,B.I., Soodyall,H., Hammer,M.F. (2005) Contrasting patterns of Y-chromosome and mtDNA variation in Africa:evidence for sex-biased demographic processes. Eur. J of Hum Genet, 13,867-876.

The archaeological and linguistic data indicate the successful colonization of Asia by Sub-Saharan Africans from Nubia 5-4k. The archaeological evidence makes it clear that around 4kya intercultural style artifacts connected Africa and Eurasia .

There is genetic, linguistic and archaeological evidence pointing to the African origin of the Dravidian speakers in India . B.B. Lal's research suggests that the Dravidian speaking people may have belonged to the C-Group of Nubia . The C-Group people spread culture from Nubia into Arabia, Iran and India as evidenced by the presence of black-and-red ware (BRW)[18] . The C-Group people used a common black and red ware that has been found from the Sudan, across Southwest Asia and the Indian Subcontinent all the way to China [19]. The

---

[18]Winters C. Origin of the Niger-Congo Speakers. WebmedCentral GENETICS 2012;3(3):WMC003149
http://www.webmedcentral.com/article_view/3149

[19] Singh, H.N. (1982)History and archaeology of Blackand Red ware. Vedic Books.net: Manchester.

Dravidian speakers in India used the same ceramics and burial procedures as the C-Group [20].

The linguistic evidence indicates a close relationship between African languages and South Eurasian languages. There is abundant evidence that the Dravidian languages are genetically related to the

Niger-Congo group [21]. A genetic linguistic relationship between the Dravidian, Elamite and Niger-Congo languages [22].

[20] Lal BB. 1963. "The Only Asian Expedition in threatened Nubia: Work by an India Mission at Afyeh and Tumas". *The Illustrated Times, London* 20 April.

[21] Aravanan, K.P. (1979) Dravidians and Africans. Madras:Paari Nilayam., and , K.P. (1980) Notable Negroid elements in Dravidian India. J Tam Stud, **17**, 20-45; Upadhyaya, P., Upadhyaya, S.P. (1979) Les liens entre Kerala et I"Afrique tels qu'ils resosortent des survivances culturelles et linguistiques. Bull. de L'IFAN,**1,** 100-132,and padhyaya, P., Upadhyaya, S.P. (1976) Affinites ethnolinguistiques entre Dravidiens et les Negro-Africain, .Bull.de L'IFAN, **1,** 127-157 ; and Winters,C. A.(1985a) "The genetic Unity between the Dravidian ,Elamite, Manding and Sumerian Languages", P Sixth ISAS ,1984, (Hong Kong:Asian Research Service) pages 1413-1425, Winters CA (1985b) The Proto Culture of the Dravidians, Manding and Sumerians. Tam Civ, 3(1),1-9 and Winters,C. A. (1989)"Tamil,Sumerian and Manding and the Genetic Model".Int J of Dra Ling,18(l): 98-127.

[22] McAlpin DW 1974. "Toward Proto Elamo Dravidian". Lang. **50(1),** 89-101 and McAlpin DW 1981. Proto Elamo Dravidian: The evidence and its implications. *Trans of the Am Philo Soc,* 71, Part 3: Philadelphia.

Balakrishnan reveals that Niger-Congo speakers and Dravidians

share identical place names[23].

The Fulani and Mandekan speak a Niger-Congo language.
Fulani and Mandekan are closely related to the Dravidian
language. The Fulani and Dravidian speaking Indians also share
many HLA factors and y-chromosomes .
It is interesting to note that in a sample of Fulani speakers,

52.8% carried the R1b haplotype . Eventhough the Fulani DNA

profile includes a high frequency of R1b they are not from the

Middle East .

```
V45                                                    R*
        M173
        R1*
                M343................................................R1b
                    P25...........................................R1b1
                        V88.....R1b1a
                                    V8..........R1b1a2
                                    V35.........R1b1a3
                                    V7....R1b1a3a
                                    V69.......R1b1a4

                                    M269*....R1b1b2
```

Figure 1: African R Haplogroups

[23] Balakrishnan,R. (2005) African roots of Dravidian-speaking Tribes: A case in Onomastics.
Internat J Dra Ling, 34, 153-202.

The archaeological, linguistic and genetic data fail to support Cruciani et al (2002,2010), contention that R1-M173 in Africa, is the result of a back migration from Asia to Africa. The phylogeography of R1-M173 in Africa makes it clear that this y-chromosome is spread globally across Africa and includes the genetic structure of diverse African populations including Berber, Chadic, Cushitic, Khoisan,Pygmy, Niger-Congo, Nilo-Saharan and Semitic speaking African populations .

Abu-Amero et al reveal that the frequency of haplotype M173 in Eurasia is as follows: Anatolia 0.19%, Iran 2.67%, Iraq 0.49% Oman 1.0%, Pakistan 0.57% and Oman 1.0% [24]. This contrast sharply with the widespread distribution of R1-M173 in Africa, that ranges between 7-95% and averages 39% . Coia et al (2005) has revealed that no maternal Eurasian lineages have been found among Sub-Saharan Africans with a R1-M173 profile.

[24]Abu-Amero,K.K., Hellani, A., Gonzalez, A.N., Larruga, J.M., Cabrera, V.M., Underhill, P.A. (2009) BMC Genetics, 10:59 doi:10.1186/1471-2156-10-59. Retrieved 04/30/2010 at: http://www.biomedcentral.com/1471-2156/10/59

Haplogroup V88 has the greatest frequency in Africa. It is predominately carried by Chadic speakers, ranges between 2-60% among Central African Niger-Congo speakers . The phylogenetically deep haplogroup R1b is mainly found in West Africa and the Sahel, where the frequency ranges between 85-100% among Niger Congo speakers .

The paternal record of M173 on the African continent illustrates a greater distribution of this y-chromosome among varied African populations than, in Asia. The greatest diversity of R1b in Africa is highly suggestive of an Africa origin for this male lineage.

Archaeological , genetic , placenames and linguistic data group linking Africans and Dravidian support the recent demic diffusion of Sub-Saharan Africans and gene flow from Africa to Eurasia. An early colonization of Eurasia 4kya by Sub-Saharan African carriers of R1-M173 is the best scenario to explain the high frequency and widespread geographical distribution of this y-chromosome on the African continent . Given the greatest diversity of R1-M173, this is the most parsimonious model explaining the frequency of R-M173 in Africa.

The Kushite people are usually associated with the C-Group civilization of Nubia and Egypt. The center of their civilization was situated first in Wawat (southern Egypt) and later Kerma. The majority of West Africans speak languages that belong to the Niger-Congo group of languages. The Niger-Congo languages originated in Nubia and were probably spoken by some of the Kushites[25].

Linguistic research make it clear that there is a close relationship between the Niger-Congo Superlanguage family and the Nilo-Saharan languages spoken in the Sudan. Heine and Nurse , discuss the Nilo-Saharan connection. They note that when Westerman described African languages he used lexical evidence to include the Nilo-Saharan and Niger-Congo languages into a Superfamily he called "Sudanic" . Using Morphological and lexical similarities Gregerson indicated that these languages belonged to a macrophylum he named " Kongo-Saharan" . Research by

---

[25]Winters C. Origin of the Niger-Congo Speakers. WebmedCentral GENETICS 2012;3(3):WMC003149
http://www.webmedcentral.com/article_view/3149

Blench reached the same conclusion, and he named this Superfamily: "Niger-Saharan" .The close relationship between Niger-Congo and Nilo-Saharan suggest an intimate relationship formerly existed between the diverse speakers of these language families, probably in Nubia.

Genetic evidence supports the upper Nile origin for the Niger-Congo speakers. Rosa et al [26], noted that while most Mande & Balanta carry the E3a-M2 gene, there are a number of Felupe-Djola, Papel, Fulbe and Mande carry the M3b*-M35 gene the same as many people in the Sudan.

In addition to haplogroup E3, we also find some carriers of haplogroup R1*-M173 in Egypt and the Sudan. In Figure 2 we observe that the majority of the carriers of y-chromosome M173 in Africa speak Niger-Congo languages. This genetic evidence makes it clear that R1*-M173 was probably carried by some C-Group speakers before they migrated out of the Upper Nile Valley

[26] Rosa A, Ornelas C, Jobling MA, Brehm A, Villems R. Y-chromosome diversit6y in the population of Guinea-Bissau: a multiethnic perspective, BMC Evol Biology 2007; 7, 124. http://www.ncbi.nlm.nih.gov/pmc/articles/PMC1976131/?tool=pubmed

region.

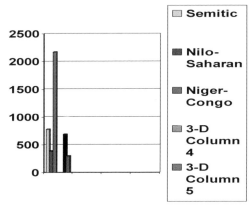

Figure 2:Frequencies of Y-Chromosome M-173 (R1b*) in Africa

Frequencies from Cruciani et al, 2010

Welmers proposed an Upper Nile homeland for the Niger-Congo speakers. He claims that they remained intact until 5000 years ago. This view is supported by linguistic and genetics evidence[27].

The Greco-Roman writers made it clear that there were two Kushite empires one in Asia and the other group in the area we call the Sudan (Hansberry,1981). The Greek writer Homer alluded

---

[27] Ibid., passim.

to the two Kushite empires, when he wrote "a race divided, whom the sloping rays; the rising and the setting sun surveys". The Greek traveler/historian Herodutus claimed that he derived this information from the Egyptians.

The Kushites were also called Ethiopians. The term Ethiopian comes from two Greek terms: Ethios 'burnt' and ops 'face', as a result Ethiopian means the 'burnt faces' . Herodutus and Homer, described these Ethiopians as "the most just of men ;the favorites of the gods" . The classical literature makes it clear that the region from Egypt to India was called by the name Ethiopia.

Hansberry[28] provides a great discussion of the evidence of African Kushites ruling in Asia and Africa. Some ancient scholars noted that the first rulers of Elam were of Kushite origin. According to Strabo, the first Elamite colony at Susa was founded by Tithnus, a King of Kush. Strabo in Book 15, Chapter 3,728

---

[28]Hansberry,L.1981. William Leo Hansberry: African History Notebook.Vol 2; and Africa & Africans as Seen by Classical Writers, (Ed.) by Joseph E. Harris. Washington,D.C.: Howard University Press.

wrote that in fact it is claimed that Susa was founded by Tithonus Memnon's father, and his citadel bore the name Memnonium. The Susians are also called Cissians. Aeschylus, calls Memnon's mother Cissia.

There is genetic, linguistic and archaeological evidence pointing to the African origin of the Dravidian speakers in India. Lal's (1963) research suggests that the Dravidian speaking people may have belonged to the C-Group. The C-Group people spread culture from Nubia into Arabia, Iran and India as evidenced by the presence of black-and-red ware (BRW). Although the Egyptians preferred the cultivation of wheat, many ancient C-Group people were agro-pastoral people who cultivated Millet/Sorghum and raised cattle. It was the Dravidians who probably took millet to India [29].

The C-Group people used a common black and red ware that has been found from the Sudan, across Southwest Asia and the

---

[29] Winters CA 2008b. African millets taken to India by Dravidians. *Ann of Bot*, http://aob.oxfordjournals.org/cgi/eletters/100/5/903#49

Indian Subcontinent all the way to China . The earliest use of this BRW was during the Amratian period (c.4000 3500 BC). The users of the BRW were usually called Kushites.In Map-Figure 4, we see the Kushite expansion from Africa to Asia.

Figure 4: Route of Kushite Expansion from Africa to Asia

The Armenians made it clear that the ancients called Persia, Media,Elam , Aria, and the entire area between the Tigris and

Indus river Kush .Bardesones, writing in his Book of the Laws of Countries, in the 2nd Century said that the "Bactrians who we called Qushani (or Kushans)" [30].The Armenians, called the earlier Parthian: Kushan and acknowledged their connection with them. Homer, Herodotus, and the Roman scholar Strabo called southern Persia AETHIOPIA . The Greeks and Romans called the country east of Kerma: Kusan.

The Kushites are associated with the C-Group people of Nubia, and the Kerma civilization. The Kushites practiced an agro-pastoral economy and they made a characteristic red-and-black pottery that they spread from Nubia to China.

Archaeologists agree that Black and red ware (BRW) indus unearth on many South India sites are related to Dravidian speaking people. The BRW style has been found on the lower levels of Madurai and Tirukkampuliyur. B.B. Lal made it clear that the South Indian BRW was related to Nubian ware dating to

---

[30] Winters,C.A.2005. Afrocentrism : Myth or Science. Lulu.com. ISBN 978-1-4116-5276-7

the Kerma dynasty. Singh made it clear that he believes that the BRW radiated from Nubia through Mesopotamia and Iran.

The legacy of the Kushites in Asia is evident in the use of their ethonym as a place-name characterized by the name Kush.

The Kushites when they migrated from Middle Africa to Asia continued to call themselves Kushites. This is most evident in place names and the names of gods. The Kassites, chief rulers of Iran occupied the central part of the Zagros . The Kassite god was called **Kashshu**, which was also the name of the people[31]. The **K-S-H**, name element is also found in India. For example **Kishkinthai**, was the name applied to an ancient Dravidian kingdom in South India. Lets not forget that the Kings of Sumer, were often referred to as the " Kings of Kush".

[31]Winters, C.A. 2000. "Memnonia ". In Shades of Memnon, Book II. Brother G (pp.13-33).SekerNefer Group,Chicago. ISBN 0-9662374-2-0

The major Kushite tribe in Central Asia was called Kushana. The Kushan of China were **Ta Yueh-ti** or "the Great Lunar Race". Along the Salt Swamp, there was a state called **Ku-Shih** of Tibet . The city of **K-san**, was situated in the direction of Kushan, which was located in the Western part of the Gansu Province of China [32].

Anatolia was occupied by many Kushite groups, including the Kashkas and Hatti. The Hatti ,like the Dravidian speaking people were probably related . The Hatti were probably members of the Tehenu tribes.

The Tehenu were composed of various ethnic groups. The Tehenu was a major African population associated with the C-Group. One of the Tehenu tribes was identified by the Egyptians as the **Hatiu** or **Haltiu**[33] .The Hatiu, may represent the Hatti tribe.

[32] Ibid., p.24.
[33] El Mosallamy,A.H.S. (1986). Libyco-Berber relations with ancient Egypt:The Tehenu in Egyptian records. In (pp.51-68), p.55; and L. Borchardt, Das Grabdenkmal des Konigs Sahure. Vol. II, Table 1.

Singer[34] has suggested that the Kaska, are remnants of the indigenous Hattian population which was forced northward by the Hittites. But at least as late as 1800 BC, Anatolia was basically settled by Hattians [35].

We can use craniometric data to understand ancient population history. The craniometric evidence indicates a process of demic diffusion of Kushite people into Mesopotamia and Anatolia between 5-4kya. Craniometric data[36] sets support a continuos dispersal modal of Sub-Saharan Africans from Africa to Eurasia between 5-4kya[37].

---

[34]Singer, I. (1981). Hittites and Hattians in Anatolia at the beginning of the Second Millennium B.C., J of Indo-Euro Stud, 9 (1-2):119-149.

[35] Steiner, G. (1981). The role of the Hittites in ancient Anatolia, J of Indo-Euro Stud, 9 (1-2): 150-169.

[36] Tomczyk,J., Jedrychowska-Danska, K., Ploszaj,T & Witas H.W. (2010). Anthropological analysis of the osteological material from an ancient tomb (Early Bronze Age) from the middle Euphrates valley, Terqa (Syria) , International Journal of Osteoarchaeology, Retrieved 04/04/10 from (www.interscience.wiley.com)DOI:10.1002/oa.1150.

[37] Ricaut,F.X. and Waelkens.2008. Cranial Discrete Traits in a Byzatine Population and Eastern Mediterranean Population Movements, Hum Biol, 80(5):535-564.

There is a positive relationship between crania from Africa and Eurasia. The archaeologist Marcel-Auguste Dieulafoy[38] and Hanberry maintains that their was a Sub-Saharan strain in Persia . These researchers maintain that it was evident that an Ethiopian dynasty ruled Elam from a perusal of its statuary of the royal family and members of the army[39]. Dieulafoy noted that the textual evidence and iconography make it clear that the Elamites were Africans, and part of the Kushite confederation[40] .Dieulafoy made it clear that the Elamites at Susa were Sub-Saharan Africans.

Marcel Dieulafoy and M. de Quatrefages observed that the craniometrics of the ancient Elamites of Susa indicate that they were Sub-Saharan Africans or Negroes .

[38]Dieulafoy, J. 2004. *The Project Gutenberg EBook of Perzi, Chaldea en Susiane*, by Jane Dieulafoy. Retrieved 04/04/10
http://www.gutenberg.org/files/13901/13901-h/13901-h.htm
[39]Dieulafoy, M.A.2010.. *L' Acropole de Suse d'après les fouilles exécutées en 1884, 1885, 1886, sous les auspices du Musée du Louvre.* Retrieved 04/04/10 from :
http://www.archive.org/stream/lacropoledesused01dieu#page/2/mode/2up

[40]Ibid., passim .

Ancient Sub-Saharan African skeletons have also been found in Mesopotamia [41]. The craniometric data indicates that continuity existed between ancient and medieval Sub-Saharan Africans in Mesopotamia [42].

There is a genetic linguistic relationship between the Dravidian, Elamite and Niger-Congo languages. The linguistic evidence makes it clear that a genetic relationship exist between Elamite and the Mande languages .

The relationship between the Mande and Elamite languages is interesting because the Garama or Garamante people of Crete, probably spoke a Mande language. Graves claimed that the Garamante formed part of the Mande group that live along the Niger River[43].

---

[41]Tomczyk,J., Jedrychowska-Danska, K., Ploszaj,T & Witas H.W. (2010). Anthropological analysis of the osteological material from an ancient tomb (Early Bronze Age) from the middle Euphrates valley, Terqa (Syria) , International Journal of Osteoarchaeology, Retrieved 04/04/10 from (www.interscience.wiley.com)DOI:10.1002/oa.1150.

[42] Ricaut,F.X. and Waelkens.2008. Cranial Discrete Traits in a Byzatine Population and Eastern Mediterranean Population Movements, Hum Biol, 80(5):535-564.

[43]Graves, R.1980. The Greek Myths. Middlesex: Penguid Book. Ltd. 2vols.

The relationship between the Elamite and Mande languages is interesting because Ricault and Waelkens (2008) noted a relationship between the Anatolia populations and Niger-Congo speakers. The Mande languages belong to the Niger-Congo Superfamily of languages. This suggest that the Garamante spoke a Niger-Congo language.

The founders of civilization on Crete were the Garamante. The Minoans called themselves Keftiu. The Egyptians recorded some Keftiu names in their hieroglyphs. These names are common clan names among the Mande speaking people [44].

Ricault and Waelkens provide craniometric and other evidence of a Cretan or Keftiu expansion into Anatolia[45]. They believe that the Cretans colonized Anatolia; and that negro skeletons come from Illion-Troy, which as we discussed earlier was founded by Kushites [46]. The research of Ricault and

---

[44] Winters,C.A. 2010. The Ancient Minoans: Keftiu were Mande Speakers . Retrieved 04/12/2010 from http://bafsudralam.blogspot.com/search?q=Minoans
[45]Ricaut,F.X. and Waelkens.2008. Cranial Discrete Traits in a Byzantine Population and Eastern Mediterranean Population Movements, Hum Biol, 80(5):535-564.

[46]Winters,C.A.2005. Afrocentrism : Myth or Science. Lulu.com

Waelkens is significant because they noted that the craniometric data set from Anatolia is related to West African (Niger-Congo) and Kerma (Kushite) populations.

Conclusion

The phylogenetic profile of R-M173 supports an ancient migration of Kushites from Africa to Eurasia as suggested by the Classical writers. In Map-Figure 3, we outline the spread of haplogrorp R from Nubia into Asia and West Africa. This expansion of an African Kushite population probably took place Neolithic period.

The accumulated Classical literature, archaeological, craniometric, genetic and linguistic evidence suggest a genetic relationship between the Kushites of Africa and Kushites in Eurasia that can not be explained by microevolutionary mechanisms. The phylogeographic profile of R1*-M173 supports this ancient migration of Kushites from Africa to Eurasia as suggested by the Classical writers. This expansion of Kushites into Eurasia probably took place over 4kya.

Figure 3: The Kushite Distribution Haplogroup R

The linguistic evidence makes it clear that the Nilo-Saharan and Niger-Congo languages are related. The genetic evidence indicates that Nilo-Saharan and Niger-Congo speakers carry the y-chromosomes M3b*-M35 and R1*-M173, an indicator for the earlier presence of speakers of this languages in an original Nile Valley homeland.

The distribution of y-chromosome specific haplogroups in areas formerly occupied by the Kushite people of Asia reveal continuity between the ancient inhabitants of Anatolia, Mesopotamia and Persia and Africa. The genetic pattern indicates a significant Sub-Saharan male contribution to the populations presently situated in south-western Eurasia.

The tradition of a Kushite migration from Africa to Asia recorded in the classical literature is supported by the clinal biological pattern of y-chromosome lineages in Africa and Eurasia. The presence of R1*-M173 among Anatolians and Iranians supports a Neolithic demic diffusion of Kushite agropastoral populations into this region. The cranial discrete traits, y-chromosome haplogroups and linguistic affiliations shared between Sub-Saharan Africans, the ancient Mesopotamian, Anatolian and Iranian populations can only be the result of a human migration from Africa to Eurasia in ancient times as noted by the Classical writers of Greece and Rome.

Chapter 3: Sumerians and Akkadians

I wish we could separate the history of the Middle East from race, but it is impossible to do so because of the desire of Eurocentrists to make Semitic speakers members of the "white" race.

The controversy surrounding the Kushite/African/Black origins of the Elamites, Sumerians, Akkadians and "Assyrians" is simple and yet complicated. It involves both the racism exhibited toward the African slaves in the Western Hemisphere and Africans generally which led to the idea that Africans had no history ; and the need of Julius Oppert to make Semites white, to accommodate the "white" ancestry of European Jews.

To understand this dichotomy we have to look at the history of scholarship surrounding the rise of Sumero-Akkadian studies. The study of the Sumerians, Akkadians. Assyrians and Elamites began with the decipherment of the cuneiform script by Henry

Rawlinson. Henry Rawlinson had spent most of his career in the Orient. This appears to have gave him an open mind in regards to history. He recognized the Ancient Model of History, the idea that civilization was founded by the Kushite or Hamitic people of the Bible.

As result, Rawlinson was surprised during his research to discover that the founders of the Mesopotamian civilization were of Kushite origin. He made it clear that the Semitic speakers of Akkad and the non-Semitic speakers of Sumer were both Black or Negro people who called themselves sag-gig-ga "Black Heads". The Sumerians called their country **Ki-en-gi**. In Rawlinson's day the Sumerian people were recognized as Akkadian or Chaldean, while the Semitic speaking blacks were called Assyrians.

Rawlinson identified these Akkadians as Turanian or Scythic people. *But he made it clear that these ancient Scythic or Turanian speaking people were Kushites or Blacks*.

A major supporter of Rawlinson was Edward Hincks. Hincks continued Rawlinson's work and identified the ancient group as Chaldeans, and also called them Turanian speakers. Hincks, though, never dicussed their ethnic origin.

A late comer to the study of the Sumerians and the Akkadians was Julius Oppert. Oppert was a German born of Jewish parents. He made it clear that the Chaldean and Akkadian people spoke different languages. He noted that the original founders of Mesopotamia civilization called themselves **Ki-en-gi** "land of the true lords". It was the Semitic speakers who called themselves Akkadians.

Assyrians called the **Ki-en-gi** people Sumiritu "the sacred language". Oppert popularized the Assyrian name Sumer, for the original founders of the civilization. Thus we have today the Akkadians and Sumerians of ancient Mesopotamia.

Oppert began to popularize the idea that the Sumerians were related to the contemporary Altaic and Turanian speaking people, e.g., Turks and Magyar (Hungarian) speaking people. He made it clear that the Akkadians were Semites like himself . To support this idea Oppert pointed out that typological features between Sumerian and Altaic languages existed. This feature was agglutination.

The problem with identifying the Sumerians as descendants from contemporary Turanian speakers resulted from the fact that Sumerian and the Turkish languages are not genetically related. As a result Oppert began to criticize the work of Hincks (who was dead at the time) in relation to the identification of the Sumerian people as Turanian following the research of Rawlinson.

It is strange to some observers that Oppert,never criticized Rawlinson who had proposed the Turanian origin of the **Ki-en-gi** (Sumerians). But this was not strange at all. Oppert did not attack Rawlinson who was still alive at the time because he knew that Rawlinson said the Sumerians were the original Scythic and Turanian people he called Kushites. Moreover, Rawlinson made it clear that both the Akkadians and Sumerians were Blacks. For Oppert to have debated this issue with Rawlinson, who deciphered the cuneiform script, would have meant that he would have had to accept the fact that Semites were Black. There was no way Oppert would have wanted to acknowledge his African heritage, given the Anti-Semitism experienced by Jews living in Europe.

Although Oppert successfully hid the recognition that the Akkadians and the Sumerians both refered to themselves as sag-gig-ga "black heads", some researchers were unable to follow the status quo and ignore this reality. For example, Francois Lenormant, made it clear, following the research of Rawlinson, that the Elamite and Sumerians spoke genetically related languages. This idea was hard to reconcile with the depiction of people on the monuments of Iran, especially the Behistun monument, which depicted Negroes (with curly hair and beards) representing the Assyrians, Jews and Elamites who ruled the area.

As a result, Oppert began the myth that the Sumerian languages was isolated from other languages spoken in the world evethough it shared typological features with the Altaic languages. Oppert taught Akkadian-Sumerian in many of the leading Universities in France and Germany. Many of his students soon began to dominate the Academe, or held chairs in Sumerian and Akkadian studies these researchers continued to perpetuate the myth that the Elamite and Sumerian languages were not related.

There was no way to keep from researchers who read the original Sumerian, Akkadian and Assyrian text that these people recognized that they were ethnically Blacks. This fact was made clear by Albert Terrien de LaCouperie. Born in France, de LaCouperie was a well known linguist and China expert. Although native of France most of his writings are in English. In the journal he published called the Babylonian and Oriental Record, he outlined many aspects of ancient history. In these pages he made it clear that the Sumerians, Akkadians and even the Assyrians who called themselves şalmat kakkadi 'black headed people", were all Blacks of Kushite origin.

Eventhough de LaCouperie taught at the University of London, the prestige of Oppert, and the fact that the main centers for Sumero-Akkadian studies in France and Germany were founded by Oppert and or his students led to researchers ignoring the evidence that the Sumerians , Akkadians and Assyrians were Black.

In summary, the cuneiform evidence makes it clear that the

Sumerians, Akkadians and Assyrians recognized themselves as Negroes: "black heads". This fact was supported by the statues of Gudea, the Akkadians and Assyrians. Plus the Behistun monument made it clear that the Elamites were also Blacks.

The textual evidence also makes it clear that Oppert began the discussion of a typological relationship between Sumerian and Turkic languages. He also manufactured the idea that the Semites of Mesopotamia and Iran, the Assyrians and Akkadians were "whites", like himself. Due to this brain washing, and whitening out of Blacks in history, many people today can look at depictions of Assyrians, Achamenians, and Akkadians and fail to see the Negro origin of these people.

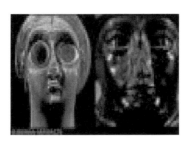

Gutian/Sumerian

To make the Sumerians "white" textbooks print pictures of artifacts dating to the Gutian rule of Lagash, to pass them off as the true originators of Sumerian civilization. No Gutian rulers of Lagash are recognized in the Sumerian King List.

Chapter 4: The Sumerians

Around 4000 to 3500 BC a group of people entered
Mesopotamia from Africa that spoke African and Semitic
languages. These people called themselves "black-heads" from
about 2000 BC to the end of Sumerian history. An Africaln
speaking group founded the Sumer Civilization.

The Sumerians and Elamites came to Mespotamia by Boats
first used in the Eastern Sahara and on the Red Sea.

The Sumerians came from Africa, like the founders of the
Indus Valley civilization. This is why their language is closely
related to African and Dravidian languages.

Researchers claim that Sumerian is not related to any other
language--this is false. The problem with many Sumerologists is
that they usually don't know, and don't bother to study any other
language to compare Sumerian too except Indo-European
languages. And since Sumerian is not related to Indo-European
they prefer to deny its relationship to African-Dravidian

languages, beacuse this would imply, thatAfrican/Dravidian/Black People founded the "first" civilization in Mesopotamia.

Rawlinson was convinced that there was a relationship between the Sumerians and Africans. As a result he used two African languages: one Semitic and the other Cushitic (Oromo) to decipher the cuneiform writing. Rawlinson was sure that the ancient Nubians and Puntites founded Mesopotamian civilization[47].

Col. Rawlinson's brother claimed that he used Oromo to decipher the cuneiform writing. If this is true we should be able to find a connection between Oromo , and the Akkadian and/or Sumerian languages. A cursory examination of Oromo and Sumerian verbs suggest that such a relationship may exist.

Sumerian	Oromo
bar 'to open' appear'	ba 'go out,
ga, aka 'to place'	kai 'to put'

[47]C.B. Rawlinson, "Notes on the early history of Babylon", Jour.Royal Asiatic Society (First Series), 15, p.230.

kur 'to rise'	ka 'to rise up'
bar 'bright, to shine'	bai 'excellent'
de 'pour'	dug 'drink'
kar 'to rise'	ka 'to rise'
dur 'sit'	tai 'sit'
kur 'enter'	gal 'enter'
pae 'appear'	ba 'appear'
bu 'perfect'	bai 'excellent'
gal 'big'	guda 'big'
gurud 'throw'	gat 'throw'
ri 'let go'	lit 'go in, enter'
du 'to plant'	dab 'to plant'
dub 'fix a boundary'	dab 'fix'

There is striking correspondence between the Oromo and Sumerian verbs. There appears to be full correspondence between the:

b-b

k-k

d-d

m-m

n-n

We also find that p/b, r/l and d/t were interchangeable

consonants in some Sumerian and Oromo words.

It is interesting that in relation to the vowels, we find that the

Sumerian –u- often appears an –a- in Oromo. e.g.:

Sumerian	Oromo
nag 'drink'	dug 'drink'
dur 'sit'	tai 'sit'
kur 'enter'	gal 'enter'
bu 'perfect'	bai 'excellent'

Granted these are only a few of the verbs found in Sumerian and

Oromo. Yet, this discussion of Oromo and Sumerian verbs

indicate that the terms illustrate cognation. This cognation in

Sumerian and Oromo verbs may explain why Rawlinson felt that

he could use Oromo in his decipherment of the cuneiform writing.

The Sumerians came from the Sahara before it became a desert. Affinities exist between Nubia ware and pottery from Ennedi and Tibesti.

These Saharan people were round-headed ancient Mediterranean type. They were often referred to as Cafsa or Capsians; a group of people not devoid of negroid characteristics according to J Desanges. Wyatt MacGaffey, claims that the term "Mediterranean" is an anthropological euphemism for "Negro".

The boats of the Saharan people are similar to those found on ancient engravings of boats in Mesopotamia and the Indus Valley. Many of the boats found in the eastern desert of Egypt and among the Red Sea Hills show affinities to Mesopotamian models.

S.N. Kramer in **The Sumerians**, claimed that Makan was Egypt, Mekluhha was Nubia-Punt, and the Indus Valley was Dilmun. Today Dilmun is believed to be found near Arabia. But the archaeological evidence suggest that the Indus Valley which was settled by Dravidian speakers was the source of the lapis lazuli , which made Dilmun famous .

Archaeological research has confirmed that cultural interaction existed between the contemporary civilizations of the 4th and 3rd millenia B.C. Extensive trade routes connected the Proto-Dravidians of the Indus Valley, with African people in Egypto-Nubia, and the Elamites and Sumerians. P. Kohl discovered that vessels from IVBI worshop at Tepe Yahya, have a uniform shape and design. Vessels sharing this style are distributed from Soviet Uzbekistan to the Indus Valley, and Sumerian, Elamite and Egyptian sites[48]. In addition, we find common arrowheads at Harappan sites, and sites in Iran, Egypt, Minoan Crete and Heladic Greece.

It appears that the locus for this distribution of cultural traditions and technology was the Saharan-Nubian zone or Kush. This would explain why the Sumerians and Elamites often referred to themselves as "ksh". For example the ancient

---

[48]). Philip L. Kohl, "The balance of trade in the mid-Third millenium BC", Current Anthropology, 19 (1978), pp.463-492.

Sumerians called their dynasty "Kish". The words "kish", "kesh" and "kush" were also names for ancient Nubia-Sudan.

The Elamites also came from Kush. According to the classical writer Strabo, Susa the centre of the Elamite civilization was founded by Tithonus, king of Kush.

B.B. Lal has shown conclusively that the Dravidians came from Nubia and were related to the C-Group people who founded the Kerma dynasty.

They both used a common black-and-red ware (BRW) which Lal found was analogous to ceramics used by the megalithic people in India who also used analogous pottery signs identical to those found in the corpus of Indus Valley writing[49].

Singh believes that this pottery spread from Nubia, through Mesopotamia and Iran southward into India[50]. The earliest examples of this BRW date to the Amratian period (c4000-3500 B.C.)[51]. This same BRW was found at the lowest levels of

---

[49] B.B. Lal, "From megalithic to the Harappan: Tracing back the graffiti on pottery", Ancient India, 16 (1960).
[50] H.N. Singh, History and Archaeology of Black-and-Red Ware, Delhi, 1982
[51] C. Winters, The Maa Civilization. 2013. Chicago: E-Createbooks.

Harappan sites at Lothal and Rangpur. After 1700 B.C. This ceramic tradition spread southward into megalithic India[52].

Dilmun was an important source of lapis lazuli. If the Indus Valley civilization was Dilmun as hypothesized by Kramer, it would explain the control of the Harappans/ or Dilmunites of this important metal.

The Indus Valley people spoke a Dravidian language[53]. The Harappans controlled the lazurite region of Badakhshan, and the routes to the tin and copper fields of central Asia[54].

The major city of the Harappans/Dilmunites in the lapis lazuli region was Shortughai. Francefort believes that many lapis lazuli works were transported to Iran and Mesopotamia from Shortughai[55]. The BRW at Shortughai is typically Harappan.

---

[52] Lal, 1960; and C.A. Winters, "The Dravido-Harappan Colonization of Central Asia", Central Asiatic Journal, 34 (1-2), pp.120-144.

[53]) C.A. Winters, "The Dravidian language of the Harappan script",Archiv Orientalni (1990).

[54] B. Brenjes, "On Proto-Elamite Iran", Current Anthropology, 24 (2) (1984), pp. 240-.
[55] Henri-Paul Franceport, "La civilisation de l'Indus aux rives de l'Oxus", Archeologie, (Decembre) p.50.

When we put all of this evidence together we must agree that there is some historical evidence for a connection between the Sumerian, Dravidian and Manding people.

The Sumerians were in control of Mesopotamia for many years. Then around 2334 BC, a group of Puntite Speakers called Akkadians under Naram-Sin or Sargon of Agade took over Mesopotamia.

This unity of the Akkadian and Ethiopian languages is supported by the Akkadians and Sumerians who claim they came from the Egypto-Nubia and Punt (Ethiopia) to west Asisa. Most modern scholar such as Joan Oates, in
Babylon suggest that Magan (Egypto-Nubia) and "Meluhha" (Punt) were southeastern Arabia and the Makian coast to as far as the Indus Valley. But according to Samuel Noah Krammer, the leading expert on the Sumerians and
Akkadians, from the time of Sargon the Great (2334 BC) down to the first millenium BC, "Magan" and "Meluhha" was Egypto-Nubia and Punt (Ethiopia) respectively. According to these records

ships from "Meluhha" and "Magan" brought trade goods to Mesopotamia.

According to W.J. Perry, in "The Growth of Civilization", the myths, legends and traditions of the Sumerians pointed to Nubia as their ancient Home. Sir Henry Rawlinson, who deciphered the cuneiform writing traced the Sumerians and Akkadians back to Nubia and Punt. Sir Rawlinson, called the ancient Mesopotamians "Kushites". It was the French Orientalist Julius Oppert, who named them Sumerians, in an attempt to make them separate from the Kushites, a Black race of Africa. But Rawlinson, called them Kushites. The name for the Sumerians was *Ki-en-gi*.

The title "King of Kish", was highly prized by subsequent Kings of Sumer as a claim of suzerainty over the whole country.

Dierelafoy, in "L'Acropole de Susa" wrote that "I shall attempt to show to what distant antiquity belongs the establishment of the Negritos upon the left bank of the Tigris and the elements constituting the Susian monarchy ....Towards 2300 BC the plains of the Tigris and Anzan Susinka were ruled by a dynasty of Negro Kings". Herodotus, who visited the area in the 5th century BC mentions the dark skin of this people who he called Ethiopians. Sir Harry Johnston, noted that the Elamites "appear to have been Negroid people with kinky hair and to have transmitted this racial type to Jews and Syrians".

The Sumerians learned all their knowledge from the Anu. The Sumerians expanded the dykes to hold back the floods of the Euphrates and Tigris rivers, and dug canals and reservoirs to store water and carry to the plains. This led to grand harvest yielding 200 and 300 grains per plant, in an area today where the Turks make a pitiful existence.

Sumerians built cities of unbaked bricks. Many of these cities such as Ur, Erudu and Uruk (Erech), Nippur, Agade (A-gaa-dee) (Akkad) have been excavated. The excavations of Erech and Agade support the Biblical accounts and skeletal remains of the ancient inhabitants of Chaldaea, show that they were Blacks. The Blacks were short with thin lips and noses.

The Ki-en-gi or Sumerians claimed that civilization in their country came there from Magan and Meluhha. The men who carried this culture and knowledge in general were called **Ab-Gal**.

Ab-Gal means 'one who leads', or 'Master of the way.'

The Sumerians said they came by sea to Sumer-Akkad. Enki, who founded Eridu situated on the head of the Persian Gulf is said to have come by sea.

The Sumerians were great navigators. They had 105 terms for various ships, which was then made of swan papyrus or other materials. Sumerians had an additional 69 terms for the manning and construction of ships.

The Sumerians spoke two different languages one was Semitic, it was used by the Semitic founders of Akkad; and the other language was Sumerian, like the Egyptians said they had come to Mesopotamia from "Magan" or Egypto-Nubia,and "Meluhha" or Punt (northeast Africa). These areas are mentioned as early as Sargon the Great and Gudea. Both countries are frequently in the Sumerian and Akkadian records.

Sargon the Great (2330) wrote that the boats of Magan, Meluhha and Dilmun were anchored in his capital of Agade. Gudea, wrote that he obtained diorite for his statues from Magan and wood for the building of temples from both Magan and Meluhha.

The Meluhhaites were called "the men of the black land" or "the black Meluhhaites". The Meluhhaites are said to have traded in carnelian, lapis lazuli, metals, stones and mineral.

Dilmun, which is believed to be the ancient Indus Valley civilization, was considered to the Paradise by the Sumerians. According to Sumerian traditions Enki, had come from Dilmun. It is interesting to note that Sumerian is closely related to the Dravidian language which was spoken in the Indus Valley in ancient times as pointed out in chapter four.

HISTORY

The most famous king of Sumer was Gilgamesh. The first king to unify much of Sumer though was Mesilim, who took the title of King of Kish around 2500 BC.

The second famous leader was Gudea. Gudea is best known for his trade expeditions and unification of Sumer. He is also said to have obtained craftsmen from Susa and Elam for the decoration of temples for his people.

By 2380 BC the Semitic people took control of Sumer. The Semitic-speakers were led by Sargon the Great. It was Sargon who unified all of Sumer.

Sargon who had once been the cup bearer of the King Ur-Zababa a king of Kish. He was a great military leader and builder of the unified state of Sumer-Akkad. The capital of his empire was "Agade", Akkad of the Bible.

By 2000 BC, the Akkadians had been subjugated by the Shubartu, a people with Indo-European names.

Also at this time Amorites entered Mesopotamia. Part of this invasion were the Canaanites who also spoke a Semitic language. The Canaanites established the rule of Hammurabi in 1800 or 1700 BC.

The fact that the Sumerians and Akkadians were Africoid or Black is best indicated by the art works from Ur, Tell Asmar, and Eridu. Indo-European rulers of Lagash and Larsa tried to imitate Sumerian styles, but many of them were Gutians and therefore not of Kushite origin. It is interesting to note that the Mesopotamia King-List, does not recognize many of the **"ensi"** of Lagash. The Gutians, ruled Lagash until Uthuhegal King of Erech conquered Tirigan the last Gutian King.

The Canaanites invaded Mesopotamia from Arabia, they occupied Palestine and Phoenicia. In the ancient literature the Canaanites were called "*Martu*"or Amorites. The most famous Canaanite ruler of Mesopotamia was Hammurabi.

Hammurabi was a great Black King. He is famous for collecting the laws of Babylon and creating a code to give justice to all Babylonians.

Another group of Canaanites, the Kassites became the rulers of Mesopotamia. The Kassites ruled for 400 years, far longer than any other Babylonian dynasty. They were very good rulers of Babylonia.

The Kassites maintained good relations with the Egyptians. This fact is supported by the Amarna cuneiform inscriptions found at the capital of Pharoah Akhenaten.

SUMERIAN SOCIETY

The Sumerian cities were led by an "***ensi",*** who was a city
governor.

Matters concerning the cities of Sumer were decided on by free-
citizens who served in an assembly, consisting of a upper house
of elders and lower house of "men".

The King of Sumer had a regular army with chariots and
armored infantry. The Sumerians cherished goodness, truth, law
and order and justice. As a result the King had to be a man who
could establish law and order and protect the poor from the rich.

The Mesopotamian cities existed only for trade and as centers
for worship. As a result the people were heavily taxed, so as to
provide income for the temples.

Land could be individually owned in Sumer-Akkad, but most
city land was owned by the temple. This land could not be
bought or sold.

CALENDAR

The Kin-en-gi were stargazers. They used the stars for both land and sea navigation and building their temples. The stars were also studied to give the Sumerians their calendar.

The Sumerians invented their own calendar. It was divided into two seasons "*emesh*" and (summer), and "*enten*" (winter). The months were lunar, they began with the evening of the new moon and lasted from 29-30 days in

length. The day began with sunset and was 12 double hours in length following the Egyptian model.

MATHEMATICS

The Babylonians had a complex mathematical system. In addition to simple arithmetic these people had algebra. Moreover they employed Pythagorean theorem more than a thousand years before the Greek Pythagoras learned it from the Egyptians. It seems though that Algebra and Geometry were just a few of the mathematical procedures used by the people of Mesopotamia.

ASTROLOGY

The Sumerians were stargazers. The Sumerians called all celestial bodies: planets, stars or constellations **MUL**, i.e., that which shines in the heights. Some **Mul,** were called **Lu Bad**, because they wandered through the heavens. The Sumerians were also familiar with Super Novas.

B. Landsberger, wrote in the Ankara University Publication that" the theory of the dynamics of heavenly bodies can only be understood as an intellectual inheritance from the Sumerians. Diodorus Siculus, writes that "the Chaldeans named the planets….in the center of their system was the sun, the greatest light of which the planets were offspring reflecting the sun's position and shine". This scientific fact was lost to Europe until Copeernicus rediscovered this reality in 1500AD.

WRITING

The Sumerians are believed to have invented their own writing system. This writing is called cuneiform, which comes from the Latin word cuneus, which means wedge. The Sumerians wrote their characters on clay with a pen

or stylus. Thousands of their tablets have been found at Nippur and Nenevah.

EDUCATION

The Sumerians or Babylonians as the Semitic/Akkadian empire was called had many schools where students learned grammar, writing,medicine and mathematics. The Sumerian schools were called: **EDUBBA**. Teachers were called **ummias** or professors.

RELIGION

The Sumerians had many gods, plus a main god called **"An"**, the heaven god. By 2500 BC with the raise of the Akkadians or Babylonians the Supreme god was called **Enlil** the air-god.

Other Sumerian gods included "Ianna" or the Akkadian goddess **"Ishtar"** and her husband the Shepard-god Dumuzi the Biblical Tammuz. The Queen of the neither world or hell was called **"Ereshkigal".**

The Babylonians had their own names of the gods. The major gods were **"Sin"** (Nanna) the mood god; **"Ishtar",** Venus; and **"Nabu"** or **"Marduk"** the god of wisdom and kwonledge. **"Nergal"** was the god of war. **"Nabu"** also the god of the scribes were popularized by them in Babylon, "Nabu" was the son of "Marduk".

Chapter 5: Elamites

The most important Kushite colony in Iran was ancient Elam.
The Elamites called their country KHATAM or KHALTAM (Ka-taam). The capital of Khaltam which we call Susa, was called
KHUZ (Ka-u-uz) by the Aryans, NIME (Ni-may) by the people of
Sumer, and KUSHSHI (Cush-she) by the Elamites.In the
Akkadian inscriptions the Elamites were called GIZ-BAM (the land
of the bow). The ancient Chinese of Bak tribesmen which
dominate China today called the Elamites KASHTI. Moreover, in
the Bible the Book of Jeremiah (xlxx,35), we read "bow of Elam".
It is interesting to note that both Khaltam-ti and Kashti as the
name for Elam, agrees with Ta-Seti, the ancient name for
Nubia/ the Meroitic Sudan.

There were already Anu people living in Iran by the time the
Proto-Saharans or Kushites began to settle West Asia. By around
3200 BC,or there abouts Kushite adventurers in search of wealth
and prestige began to settle Iran. They were able to take these

lands over because the former rulers of the land the Anu had suffered a decline in their influence in this area after the great flood which seems to have wiped out much of their civilization after 4000 BC.

The Kushites in Elam early settled the Susiana plains of southwestern Iraq and Uruk in Mesopotamia. They already arrived with their own writing and boats. It would appear that a trading network already existed in this region because the Proto-Elamites abandoned the Proto-Saharan script and used the cuneiform script which like the Egyptian hieroglyphics was probably invented by the Anu people. Since the merchants in much of West Asia were already using cuneiform, it was most logical for the Kushites to continue to use this writing so they could dominate trade in this region.

The ancients were sure the Kushites had founded the Elamite civilization. According to Strabo, the Roman geographer the first Elamite colony of Susa, was founded by Tithonus, a King of Kush, and father of Memnon. Strabo in Book 15,chapter 3,728, wrote that "In fact, it is claimed that Susa was founded by Tithonus

Memnon's father, and that his citadel bore the name Memnonium. The Susians are also called Cissians; and Aeschylus, calls Memnon's mother Cissia.Some scholars believe that Amenhotep III, may be Memnon.

Although this is the opinion of some researchers the fact that the ancient writers made it clear that Memnon came from Kush, suggest that he was not an Egyptian. It is more likely that Memnon's ancestors had lived in the Proto-Sahara. This fact is supported by the Elamite language which is clearly related to Dravidian and Manding.

A tomb of Memnon, is reported to have been formerly established in Troad, an area near Troy in northwest Anatolia, according to Martin Bernal, in volume II of BLACK ATHENA. This tomb was associated with Memnoides or Black Birds. This identification of Memnon with Black birds suggest that he was a member of the bird clan, which also founded the Shang dynasty.It should also be remembered that it was from Elam that the Manding and Dravidian explorers of Central Asia and China first made their way into East Asia.

The Elamites established an extensive trade network which linked them to the   Sumerians in the West, and the Proto-Dravidian and Mande speaking groups of Central Asia and the Indus Valley. They also had trade relations with Africa.

Archaeologists use ceramics to identify cultures. The ceramic style from Susa and Godin, parallel the ceramic inventory at Warka IV and Nippur XV in Mesopotamia. Moreover a distinctive style of chlorite (steatite) bowl manufactured at Yahya, with identically carved motifs have been discovered at excavated sites of Sumerian Early Dynasty II/III city.

The French historian Lenormant, observed that when the archaeologist Dieulafoy excavated Susa, he found that "the master of the citadel , is black; it is thus very possible that Elam was the prerogative of a black dynasty and if one refers to the characteristics of the figures already found, of an Ethiopian dynasty".

Henry Rawlinson used the Book of Genesis to find <u>the identity</u>

of the Mesopotamia. He made it clear that the original inhabitants

of Babylonia were represented by the name Nimrod and were

represented by the family of Ham: Kushites, Egyptians and etc.

This name came from the popularity among these people of

hunting the leopard (Nimri). And as noted in earlier post the

Egyptian and Nubian rulers always associated leopard spots with royalty, just as Siva is associated with the feline. As a result, Rawlinson used an African language Galla/Oromo, to decipher the cuneiform writing.

The Sumerians and Elamites came from Africa, like the founders of the Indus Valley civilization. This is why the Elamite and Sumerian languages are closely related to African and Dravidian languages.

The Kushites when they migrated from Middle Africa to Asia continued to call themselves Kushites. This is most evident in place names and the names of gods. The Kassites, chief rulers of Iran occupied the central part of the Zagros. The Kassite god was called Kashshu, which was also the name of the people. The K-S-H, name element is also found in India. For example Kishkinthai, was the name applied to an ancient Dravidian kingdom in South India. Also it should be remembered that the Kings of Sumer, were often referred to as the " Kings of Kush".

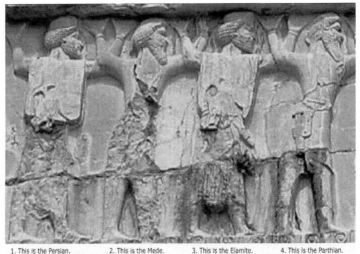

1. This is the Persian.   2. This is the Mede.   3. This is the Elamite.   4. This is the Parthian.

The major Kushite tribe in Central Asia was called Kushana.

The Kushan of China were styled Ta Yueh-ti or "the Great Lunar

Race". Along the Salt Swamp, there was a state called Ku-Shih of

Tibet. The city of K-san, was situated in the direction of Kushan,

which was located in the Western part of the Gansu Province of

China.

FIG. 94. — OFFICIER DE LA GARDE PERSE
BAS-RELIEF ÉGYPTIEN.

The Elamites later conquered Sumer. They called this line of

Kings,he "King of Kish'.

This term has affinity to the term Kush,that was given to the

Kerma dynasty, founded by the C-Group people of Kush. It is

interesting to note that the Elamite language, is closely related to

the African languages including Egyptian and the Dravidian

languages of India.

The ancients were sure the Kushites had founded the Elamite civilization. According to Strabo, the Roman geographer the first Elamite colony of Susa, was founded by Tithonus, a King of Kush, and father of Memnon. Strabo in Book 15,chapter 3,728, wrote that "In fact, it is claimed that Susa was founded by Tithonus Memnon's father, and that his citadel bore the name Memnonium. The Susians are also called Cissians; and Aeschylus, calls Memnon's mother Cissia.

The most important Kushite colony in Iran was Elam. The Elamites like other Africans practiced the custom of matrilineal descent.

The history of Elam is usually divided into three periods the Kings of Awan, Kings of Simashki and the Sukkalmah period. For over 300 years the Elamite Kings of Awan ruled Elam, and much of Mesopotamia.Much of this period is unknown.

During the 3rd Millennium B.C., the Elamites and **Su** people (a term used for mountain people in the Western Zagros) sacked Ur. The King of the **Dynasty of Simaskhi**, led to Elamite rule in Sumer. The first king of the Simashki Dynasty was Girnamme.

In Sumer, the Elamites contributed nuch to Sumerian civilization. The Elamite Kings of Sumer were called the Kings of Kish.

After a Sumerian King of Kish pushed the Elamites out of Mesopotamia, Elam went into a period of chaos until around 2500 B.C., when King Peli became the ruler of Elam. After Peli, there were six other Elamite Kings until Elam was conquered by Sargon of Akkad.

Before the **Sukkalmah period** (c.1900-1500 B.C.) much of what we know about Elam comes from the Akkadian sources. This period is called the Sukkalmah period, because the rulers of Elam were called Sukkalmah 'grand regent". The Elamite title for king was **sunkir**.

During the Sukkahmah Dynasty there was a tripartite system of rule. The Susa text indicate that there was a senior ruler called sukkalmah 'grand regent' of Elam and Shimashki, he was usually the brother of the sukkahmah, and a junior co-regent, entitled sukkal of Susa. This nephew was usually from the maternal side of the King's family. Thus the sukkal of Susa was often called the ruhusak 'sister's son'

The first rulers of the Sukkamah period was Eabarat (=Eparti). He was followed by the ruhusak Addahushu, the "sukkal and magustrate of the people of Susa". He is known mostly for his building of several temples and the erection of his "justic stele" outlining the laws of Elam .

The Elamites/Old Persians were probably descendants of the Mande people. This is obvious in the language and names of the Elamite Kings. I hope you remember the book Roots, the main character **Kunte Kinte**. His name is interesting because we have the following ruler during the Sukkalmah Dynasty: **Kutur-Nahhunte** I (c. 1752) who conquered southern Babylonia The name Kutur Nahhunte, would correspond to a popular Mande name Kunte among the Mande speaking people. The Elamite name Peli, is also popular among the Mande, in the form of Pe, this name was also common among the Olmec people of ancient

Mexico.

It should also be noted that the Mande term for people is Si, this corresponds to the word Su, used to designate the mountain people of Elam. The Elamite term Su would correspond to the Mande termSi-u (the /u/ is the plural suffix in the Mande language).

By the 2nd Millennium B.C., a new more aggressive dynasty appeared in Elam. The Kings of this Dynasty called themselves 'divine messenger, father and king' of Susa and Anzan. One of the rulers of this Dynasty was Shutruk-Nahhunte. Shutruk-Nahhunte, like Kutur invaded Mesopotamia and took Babylon around 1160B.C.

After Kutur took Babylon, the Elamites ruled Babylon until Hammurabi defeated the Elamite King Rin-Sin. Later the Elamites were driven from Larsa and other Sumerian cities back to the Susiana plains.

Chapter 6: MEDIANS

The original Proto- Saharan tribes of Central Asia were known as the Kushana, Yuehshih, Mandaga (Manda > Mande), and Kasu. The four kingdoms of Saka were the Maga (Manga), Masaka, Mansa and Mandaga (Manda). The term Saka, now used to describe a late Indo-European group that conquered Central Asia formerly was used to refer to the Kushites/Proto-Saharans of ancient

Central Asia. The name Maga, reminds us of the Magians or Maka, of the Persian inscriptions who lived in Media.

The ancient Sumerian name for Medea ,was Mada. One of the six tribes of Mada,was the "Mages" or "Magu" in Persian. The name Mage signified "the great,the High". Herodotus, claimed the the Medes came from Athens. This would support a Mande origin.

Many cities of eastern Greece were early settled by the Manding speakers who presently live in West Africa. Moreover, in the Manding languages "Maga" means 'great". Moreover, the name of the King of the Soninke (Manding) speaking empire of Ghana (300 BC to AD 1100) was called Manda.

The Magians or Medians, were probably descendants of the Manding tribes which also included the Garamantes of European and Libyan fame, and in Asia under the name of Mandaga/Medians. This view is supported by linguistic, historical and cultural data.

The language of the Medes, like Elamite is genetically related to the Manding languages. In addition the term Mandaga agrees with the title of the Manding tribes: for example, Manda agrees with Mande.

Chapter 7: ADVANCED CIVILIZATIONS IN ASIA

HATTIANS

In Asia Minor an important civilizing element in this area in Asia
Minor were the Hatti. The Hattians were blacks.

The Hattians rode chariots and used the bow. They had wonderful
architecture and believed in many gods.

Hatti

In the ancient literature the Proto Dravidians are called
Kushites. Using boats the Kushites moved down ancient
waterways many now dried up, to establish new towns in Asia
and Europe after 3500 BC. The Kushites remained supreme
around the world until 1400 1200 BC. During this period the Hua
(Chinese) and Indo European (I E) speakers began to conquer
the Kushites whose cities and economies were destroyed as a
result of natural catastrophes which took place on the planet

between 1400 1200 BC. Later, after 500 AD, Turkish speaking people began to settle parts of Central Asia. This is the reason behind the presence of the K s h element in many place names in Asia e.g., Kashgar, HinduKush, and Kosh. The HinduKush in Harappan times had lapis lazuli deposits.

Mother and Child, probably Hattic, Anatolia - 2000B.C.

Proto Saharans/Kushites expanded into Inner Asia from two primary points of dispersal : Iran and Anatolia. In Anatolia the

Kushites were called Hattians and Kaska. In the 2nd millennium BC, the north and east of Anatolia was inhabited by non I E speakers.

Anatolia was divided into two lands "the land of Kanis" and the "land of Hatti". The Hatti were related to the Kaska people who lived in the Pontic mountains.

Hattians lived in Anatolia. They worshipped Kasku and Kusuh. They were especially prominent in the Pontic mountains. Their sister nation in the Halys Basin were the Kaska tribes. The Kaska and Hattians share the same names for gods, along with personal and place names[56] . The Kaska had a strong empire which was never defeated by the Hittites.

Singer has suggested that the Kaska, are remnants of the indigenous Hattian population which was forced northward by the Hittites. But at least as late as 1800 BC, Anatolia was basically

---

[56]Itamar Singer, Hittites and Hattians in Anatolia at the beginning of the Second Millennium B.C., Journal of Indo-European Studies, 9 (1-2) (1981), pp.119-149.

settled by Hattians [57].

Anatolia was occupied by many Kushite groups, including the Kashkas and or Hatti. The Hatti , like the Dravidian speaking people were probably related . The Hatti were probably members of the Tehenu tribes.

The Tehenu was composed of various ethnic groups. One of the Tehenu tribes was identified by the Egyptians as the Hatiu or Haltiu.

During the Fifth Dynasty of Egypt (2563-2423), namely during the reign of Sahure there is mention of the Tehenu people. Sahure referred to the Tehenu leader "Hati Tehenu" [58].(3) These Hatiu, may correspond to the Hatti speaking people of Anatolia. The Hatti people often referred to themselves as Kashkas or Kaskas.

The Hatti controlled the city state of Kussara. Kussara was situated in southern Anatolia.

---

[57] Gerd Steiner, The role of the Hittites in ancient Anatolia, Journal of Indo-European Studies, 9 (1-2) (1981), 119-149.

[58] El Mosallamy,A.H.S. Libyco-Berber relations with ancient Egypt:The Tehenu in Egyptian records. In (pp.51-68) 1986, p.55; and L. Borchardt, Das Grabdenkmal des Konigs Sahure. Vol. II, Table 1.

The earliest known ruler of Kussara was Pitkhanas. It was his son Anitta (c. 1790-1750 BC) who expanded the Kussara empire through much of Anatolia.

Many researchers get the Hittites (Nesa) mixed up with the original settlers of Anatolia called Hatti according to Steiner ".[T]his discrepancy is either totally neglected and more or less skillfully veiled, or it is explained by the assumption that the Hittites when conquering the country of Hatti adjusted themselves to the Hattians adopting their personal names and worshipping their gods, out of reverence for a higher culture" [59].

Neshili, was probably spoken by the Hatti, not the IE Hittite. Yet, this language is classified as an IE langauge. Researchers maintain that the Hatti spoke 'Hattili' or Khattili "language of the Hatti", and the IE Hittites spoke "Neshumnili"/ Neshili . Researchers maintain that only 10% of the terms in Neshumnili is IE. This supports the view that Nesumnili may have been a lingua franca.

---

[59]Steiner, p.160

It is clear that the Anatolians spoke many languages including:Palaic, Hatti, Luwian and Hurrian, but the people as you know mainly wrote their writings in Neshumnili [60]. The first people to use this system as the language of the royal chancery were Hatti Itamar Singer makes it clear that the Hittites adopted the language of the Hatti [61]. Steiner wrote that, " In the complex linguistic situation of Central Anatolia, in the 2nd Millennium B.C. with at least three, but probably more different languages being spoken within the same area there must have been the need for a language of communication or lingua franca [i.e., Neshumnili), whenever commercial transactions or political enterprises were undertaken on a larger scale" [62].

The Hatti language which provided the Hittites with many of the terms Indo-Aryan nationalists use to claim and Aryan origin for the Indus civilization is closely related to African languages including Egyptians. For example Big, mighty, powerful protect,

---

[60] I.M. Diakonoff and P.L. Kohl, Early Antiquity. Chicago: University of Chicago Press, 1990
[61] . Itamar Singer, Hittites and Hattians in Anatolia at the Beginning of the Second Millennium BC,Journal of Indo-European Studies, 9 (1-2) (pp.119-149).

[62] Ibid., p.162

help upper :

Hattic ur $uh tufa

Egyptian wr swh tp

Malinke fara solo dya, tu 'raising'

Head stretch (out) prosper to pour

Hattic tu put falfalat duq

Egyptian tup pd

Malinke tu 'strike head' pe, bemba fin'ya du

Eye hand Place King, term of respect

The Malinke-Bambara and Hatti language share other cognates and grammatical features. For example,in both languages the pronoun can be prefixed to nouns, e.g., Hatti le 'his', **le fil** 'his house'; Malinke-Bambara a 'his', a falu 'his father's house'. Other Hatti and Malinke- Bambara cognates include:

Hattic **b'la ka -ka Kaati**

Malinke **n'ye teke -ka ka**, **kuntigi** 'headman'

Good hypothesis generation suggest that given the fact that the Malinke-Bambara and Hatti languages share cognate terms, Sumerian terms may also relate to Hatti terms since they were also Kushites. Below we compare a few Hatti, Sumerian and Malinke Bambara terms:

Mother father lord,ruler build, to set up

Hattic na-a ša tex

Malinke na baba sa te

Sumerian na 'she' aba tu 'to create'

To pour child,son up, to raise strength,powerful land

Hatti dug pin,pinu tufa ur -ka

Malinke du den dya, tu fara -ka

Sumerian dub peš dul usu ki

Conclusion

In summary, the Hattic speaking people were members of the Kushite tribe called Tehenu. They were probably called Hati (pl. Hatiu), by the Egyptians.

   The language of the Hittites was more than likely a lingua franca, with Hattic, at its base. In Western Anatolia many languages were spoken including Hattic, Palaic, Luwian and

Hurrian used Nesa as a lingua franca. **For example, the king of Arzawa, asked the Egyptian in the Amarna Letters, to write them back in Nesumnili rather than Egyptian**[63] .

Steiner notes that "In the complex linguistic situation of Central Anatolia in the 2nd Millennium B.C., with at least three, but probably more different languages being spoken within the same area there must have been the need for a language of communication or lingua franca whenever commercial transaction or political enterprises were undertaken on a larger scale"[64] .

This led Steiner to conclude that "moreover the structure of Hittite easily allowed one to integrate not only proper names, but also nouns of other languages into the morphological system. Indeed, it is a well known fact the vocabulary of Hittite is strongly interspersed with lexemes from other languages, which is a phenomenon typical of a "lingua franca"[65] .

---

[63] Ibid., p.161.
[64] Ibid., p.162
[65] Ibid., p.161

Hurrians

Hurrians is closely related to the Dravidian group of languages.

An important group in Anantolia in addition to the Hatti, were the Hurrians. The Hurrians enter Mesopotamia from the northeastern hilly area . They introduced horse-drawn war chariots to Mesopotamia .

Hurrians penetrate Mesopotamia and Syria-Palestine between 1700-1500 BC. The major Hurrian Kingdom was Mitanni, which was founded by Sudarna I (c.1550), was established at Washukanni on the Khabur River. The Hurrian capital was Urkesh, one of its earliest kings was called Tupkish.

Mitanni

Linguistic and historical evidence support the view that Dravidians influenced Mittanni and Lycia.

Most of what we know about Hurrian comes from theTel al-Armarna letters. These letters were written to the Egyptian pharaoh. These letters are important because they were written in a language different from diplomatic Babylonian.

The Hurrians spoke a non-IE language. Formerly, linguist suggested that the Hurrians were dominated by Indic speakers. Linguist of the Indo-Iranian languages were found of this theory because some of the names for the earliest Indo-Aryan gods:

Hurrian	Sanscrit
Mi-it-ra	Mitra
Aru-na	Varuna
In-da-ra	Indra

Indo-Aryan terms for chariots and horsemenship are found in Hurrian. This made the Indo-Aryan domination of Hurrians good support for an Anatolia origin for the IE speakers.

This theory held high regards until Bjarte Kaldhol studied 500 Hurrian names and found that only 5, were Indo-Aryan sounding. This made it clear that the IA people probably learned horsemenship from the Hurrians, and not the other way around.

The Kurds are IE speakers. They may have preceeded to the Turkish speakers in the area but they are not related to the Hurrians. The Hurrians were probably Kushites, or Black people, like the Hatic and Kaska tribes.

An important group in Anantolia in addition to the Hatti, were the Hurrians. The Hurrians enter Mesopotamia from the northeastern hilly area . They introduced horse-drawn war chariots to Mesopotamia .

Hurrians penetrate Mesopotamia and Syria-Palestine between 1700-1500 BC. The major Hurrian Kingdom was Mitanni, which was founded by Sudarna I (c.1550), was established at Washukanni on the Khabur River. The Hurrian capital was Urkesh, one of its earliest kings was called Tupkish.

Linguistic and historical evidence support the view that Dravidians influenced Mittanni and Lycia. Alain Anselin is sure that Dravidian speaking peoples once inhabited the Aegean. For example Anselin has discussed many Dravidian place names found in the Aegean Sea area.

Two major groups in ancient Anatolia were the Hurrians and

Lycians. Although the Hurrians are considered to be Indo-European speakers, some Hurrians probably spoke a Dravidian language.

The Hurrians lived in Mittanni. Mittanni was situated on the great bend of the Upper Euphrates river. Hurrian was spoken in eastern Anatolia and North Syria.

Most of what we know about Hurrian comes from the Tel al-Armarna letters. These letters were written to the Egyptian pharaoh. These letters are important because they were written in a language different from diplomatic Babylonian.

The letters written in the unknown language were numbered 22 and 25. In 1909 Bork, in Mitteilungen der Vorderasiatische Gesellschaft, wrote a translation of the letters.

In 1930, G.W. Brown proposed that the words in letters 22 and 25 were Dravidian especially Tamil. Brown (1930), has shown that the vowels and consonants of Hurrian and Dravidian are analogous. In support of this theory Brown (1930) noted the following similarities between Dravidian and Hurrian: 1) presence of a fullness of forms employed by both languages; 2) presence of active and passive verbal forms are not distinguished; 3)

presence of verbal forms that are formed by particles; 4)

presence of true relative pronouns is not found in these

languages; 5) both languages employ negative verbal forms; 6)

identical use of -m, as nominative; 7) similar pronouns; and 8)

similar ending formations:

Dravidian Hurrian

a a

-kku -ikka

imbu impu

There are analogous Dravidian and Hurrian terms:

English Hurrian Dravidian

mountain paba parampu

lady,woman aallay ali

King Sarr,zarr Ca, cira

god en en

give tan tara

to rule irn ire

father attai attan

wife,woman asti atti

Many researchers have noted the presence of many Indo-Aryan words. In Hurrians. This has led some researchers to conclude that Indo –Europeans may have ruled the Hurrians. This results from the fact that the names of the Hurrian gods are similar to the Aryan gods:

Hurrian Sanskrit

Mi-it-va Mitra

Aru-na Varuna

In-da-ra Indra

Na-sa-at-tiya Nasatya

There are other Hurrian and Sanskrit terms that appear to show a relationship:

English Hurrian Sanskrit Tamil

One aika eka okka 'together'

Three tera tri

Five panza panca añcu

Seven satta sapta

Nine na nava onpatu

Other Hurrian terms relate to Indo-Aryan:

English Hurrian I-A Tamil

Brown babru babhru pukar

Grey parita palita paraitu 'old'

Reddish pinkara pingala puuval

English Mitanni Vedic Tamil

Warrior marya marya makan, maravan

Although researchers believe that the Hurrians-Mitanni were dominated by Indo-Aryans this is not supported by the evidence. Bjarte Kaldhol found that only 5 out of 500 Hurrian names were I-A sounding .

The linguistic evidence discussed above is consistent with the view that the only Indian elements in Anatolian culture were of Dravidian ,rather than Indo-Aryan origin. This evidence from Mittanni adds further confirmation to the findings of N. Lahovary in Dravidian Origins and the West, that prove the earlier presence of Dravidian speakers in Anatolia.

This data also makes it clear that the Dravidians was one of the Kushites tribes that formerly lived in Anatolia.

HITTITES

Armed with iron weapons a group of Indo-European speaking Nomads the

Hittites, slowly settled parts of Asia Minor. These Hittites armed with

iron weapons later conquered the Hattians and adopted their religion, horse

drawn chariots, and architecture. The Hittites ruled Asia Minor from

1600-1200 BC.

PHOENICIANS

Along the Eastern Mediterranean there was a group of small City-States

in an area called Phoenicia. These people called themselves Canaanites, but

in history they are known by the name given them by the Greeks: Phoenicians.

The Major Phoenician cities were Byblos, Sidon and Tyre. They were

known as master sea merchants and ship builders.

The Phoenicians were great sailors. They established colonies as far away as Britain, Italy, Spain and North Africa. In the 600 BC they sailed

around Africa.

.

Chapter 8: ASSYRIANS AND PERSIANS

Asia Minor and Mesopotamia were ruled by blacks until 1500

BC. Indo-European speaking nomads began to migrate into

these areas due to severe living conditions in Europe and Asia

Minor, and by 1200 BC they began to

rule many areas formerly ruled by blacks.

The period of small independent states in Mesopotamia ended

in 1100 BC, when the Assyrians came to power.

By 900 BC a mixed group of people called Assyrians, who had

lived in the mountains invaded Babylon. The Assyrians invented a

battering ram chariot which could break down walls. This new

technology helped them to take over Mesopotamia.

The homeland of the Assyrians was the highland area of the

North Upper Tigris River. The Assyrians soon conquered

many neighboring states including Babylonia in 747 BC, Israel in

722 BC, and Phoenicia 701 BC.

The Assyrians introduced the minting coins and the idea of buying goods on credit. The Assyrians led by Tiglath-Pileser's son Shalmanser (726-722) seized the throne in Babylon. Upon taking the throne he took the name Sargon.

Relief from the palace of King Sargon II in Dur-Sharrukin, circa 700 B.C.

Under Sargon, the Assyrians founded an empire extending from Babylon through Palestine even up to the gates of Egypt. Sargon died in battle.

Assyrian Soldiers

The Assyrians may have been of African origin. Much of the oral traditions of the Arabs mentioned that the Soninke (Mande speakers) were descendants of the Persians. Moreover, it is interesting to note that the SouSou of West Africa , may be related to the Assyrians who were called

Sousou and Sousi.

The Assyrians ruled their empire thru a well-organized system of government and well trained army. Their empire made up the entire fertile crescent.

Assyrian king Sennacherib

They used iron weapons, and charioteers to smash their enemies. Conquered people were harshly treated. The Assyrians were cruel rulers, often beheading or burning alive subject people. There was very little freedom and the conquered people had no self government.

The capital of the Assyrian empire was Nineveh. At the library of Nineveh many text written on clay tablets have been found. In 612 BC the Assyrians were conquered by the Chaldeans.

CHALDEANS

The Chaldean or Neo-Babylonian empire re-introduced fine arts, and civilization to Mesopotamia. Led by King Nebuchadnezzar, the Chaldeans conqurered much of the Fertile Crescent.

Chaldean close-up

The Chaldeans made Babylon into the most famous hanging gardens, which the Greeks said was one of the seven wonders of the world. He is also responsible for the building the ziggurate or temple tower, in honor of Murduk the chief god. Many scholars believe the Bible story of the Tower of Babel, is the result of the ziggurate.

They adopted the calendar and mathematics of the Sumerians to study the stars and contribute to the study of astronomy. They used astrology to foretell the future.

PERSIANS

Soon after the death of Nebuchadnezzar in 562 BC, Babylon began to decay. Soon the Persians conquered the Medes and Chaldeans and became the most powerful State in Asia Minor.

William Leo Hansberry gives a great discussion of the evidence of African Kushites ruling in Asia and Africa. Hansberry, in the **African History Notebook** Volume 2 noted that: "In Persia the old Negroid element seems indeed to have been sufficiently powerful to maintain the overlord of the land. For the Negritic strain is clearly evident in statuary depicting members of the royal family ruling in the second millenium B.C.Hundreds of years later, when Xerxes invaded Greece, the type was well represented in the Persian army. In the remote mountain regions bordering on Persia and Baluchistan, there is to be found at the present time a Negroid element which bears a remarkable resemblance to the type represented on the ancient mounments. Hence the Negritic or Ethiopian type has proved persistent in this area, and in ancient times it seems to have constituted numerically and socially an important factor in the population" (p.52) .

Ruling from Persepolis the Persians had early defeated the Elamites. The Persians also conquered the Assyrians.

The Persians spoke Old Persian which was Elamite. The ancient Persians wrote in Elamite. Aryan is not an ethnonyn. Aryan just means nobel.

The people ruling Iran today are not Persians. They do not

speak the Persian languages.

The Classical writers said the Elamites were Kushites.
I believe the Kushites introduced Eb3 to Eurasia. Luis, et. al argue that the **presence of Egyptian lineage (E3b1-M78)(c.7.8kya) is consistent with northbound migrations of this haplotype - thru the levant - reflected in M78 males as far north as Turkey (c.4.8kya)** .In Asia the Kushites were called Kushiya.

The decipherer of the cuneiform writing of Mesopotamia, Rawlinson, said Puntites and Kushites were established in Asia. He found mention of Kushiya and Puntiya in the inscriptions of Darius. He also made it clear that the name Kush was also applied to southern Persia, India, Elam, Arabia, and Colchis (a part of southern Russia/Turkistan) in ancient times.

In Persia the old Negroid element seems indeed to have been sufficiently powerful to maintain the overlord of the land. For the Negritic strain is clearly evident in statuary depicting members of the royal family ruling in the second millenium B.C.

Under Cyrus the Great, beginning in 550 BC, the Persians

became a world power. At the death of Cyrus, the Persian empire

extended from the Agean Sea, east to India, and south to Egypt.

It was under Cyrus all the citizens of the Empire was welcomed to

contribute to Persian civilization.

Overtime Persian empire began to decrease in size. The son

of Cyrus took control of Egypt. But the Kushites of Kerma/Nubia

destroyed most of his army when he tried to invade Kush

The Persians were less cruel than the Assyrians. They gave the conquered people limited political freedom, equal rights and responsibilities. The defeated people also were able to worship their own gods, practice their own religion, customs and language.

Darius I, ruled Persia while it was a large empire. He was a "despot" a person having unlimited power.

Darius I of Persia

Each district or "satrap" was governed by the king's representative. To check on the governors, the king employed inspectors called "THE EYES AND EARS OF THE KING", to check on the condition of the land and people in the particular satrap they must inspect.

To enhance communication, the Persian kings made fine network of roads. The kings messengers rode along these roads on horseback. They changed horses every 14 miles.

A money system of gold and silver was used in the empire. The tax burden was fair, and the king protected farming and helped trade.

The religion of the Persians was Zorastrinism. This religion called on people to worship Ahura Mazda the god of Good. Ahura Mazda, was suppose to one day defeat the god of evil Ahriman and the wicked would go to hell, while the followers of Ahura Mazda would enter heaven. This religion founded by Zoroaster in the 7th century BC, encouraged the Persian kings to be merciful.

The Persians were later subjugated by the Greeks led by Alexander the Great.

Chapter 9: The Anu People of India

The Anu people spread into India and Southeast Asia 12kya. Today there are few Anu living in Southeast Asia. Most Anu live in India and the Annamese Islands. In India they are called Munda people [66].

The Munda live in North India among varying populations and linguistic groups. Researchers have assumed that the Munda represented the earliest Indian population. This theory has been recently disputed by researchers who claim a S.E. Asian origin for the Munda speakers. The S.E. Asian origin hypothesis is not supported by Munda mtDNA phylogeny, archaeology and linguistics. This evidence suggest an ancient presence of Munda

[66] Clyde Winters (2011) Munda Speakers are the Oldest Population in India. *The Internet Journal of Biological Anthropology.* 4 (2) Retrieved 9/21/2011
http://www.ispub.com/journal/the_internet_journal_of_biological_anthropology/volume_4_number_2_61/article/munda-speakers-are-the-oldest-population-in-india.html

speakers in India before the Dravidian and Indo-Aryan speaking populations.

The HUGO Pan-Asian SNP Consortium has done much to bring the genetic data for India in line with the archaeological, anthropological and linguistic data[1]. The archeological evidence indicated that the first settlers of India were probably Austro-Asiatic (Munda) speakers , then Dravidian speakers and finally Southeast Asians speakers [2-3].

There are three branches of Austro-Asiatic (AA): Munda, Mon-Khmer and Nicobarese. The Munda are classified into Southern and Northern branches situated in Central and Eastern India. The Khasi-Aslian speakers live in the Meghalaya state.

Although Chaubey et al argue for a SE Asian origin for the Munda speakers the linguistic and genetic data fails to support this conclusion[4]. The linguistic evidence makes it clear that eventhough Munda is placed in the AA Superfamily it is recognized as a separate branch[5].

The AA languages probably originated in India [5-6]. The present linguistic evidence suggest that AA spread from northeast India to Myanmar and Bangladesh.

Moreover, as noted by Blench linguist have not been able to reconstruct proto-Austro-Asiatic [7]. Given the lack of an abundance of cognate terms within AA we can not truly describe the relationship between the members of this language family as a genetic linguistic relationship.

The Munda languages are very old. South Munda dates to 18.4ky +-2.4ky. The age of Indian Khasi-Aslian is 10.6+- 1.6ky, while Munda generally dates to 12.4+-1.3ky [8].

The Munda share similar biological backgrounds with other Indian speakers [9]. Yet, the genetic evidence also indicates that the Munda homeland, can not be determined solely on the ancestral home of speakers of Southeast Asian languages, including Khasi Aslian. This is supported by the large genetic variance found among and within Munda speakers [10].

Chaubey et al argues that because the phylogeography of mtDNA R7 and y-chromosome marker M95 specific to O2a is found among Khasi-Aslian speakers, the Munda speakers

probably originated in Southeast Asia (SEA)[4]. But Chaubey et al

admit that there is a clear distinction between the Munda and

Southeast Asian Khasi-Aslian speaking groups yet they place the

origin of Munda speakers in SEA[4]. For example, Chaubey et al

generally found that the PC-s clustered the Munda with Dravidian

speakers, rather than the Khasi-Aslian speakers who are closer

to Southeast Asian populations[4]

The mtDNA of Munda speakers show a deep rooted

ancestry in India. The Munda specific mtDNA haplogroups include

M40a, M45, R7 and R6a. The Munda speakers cluster

predominately in R7. The spread of R7 is centered within the AA

"heartland" [11].

Complete mtDNA sequence based typology discovered the

deep rooted R7al subclade. The presence of R7a1 among Indo-

European and Dravidian speakers probably is the result of their

living in close proximity to AA speakers is bet explained by

language shift given the antiquity of y-chromosome O2.

Thangaraj et al using coalescence time and archaeological evidence illustrated that the TRMCA for mtDNA R8 which is found among Munda speakers have the following dates : R8 (41.7 kya), R8a (15.4 kya) and R8b (27.7 kya)[13] . The dating for mtDNA R8 indicates that this haplogroup and R7 are probably autochthonus to India.

The mtDNA of Munda speakers also includes deep rooted haplogroups from macrohaplogroup M. In addition to mtDNA haplogroup M2, we also find M58, M31, M6a2 and M42 among Munda speakers.

The Munda y-chromosome is O2a (M95). Kumar reports a coalescent rate of 65kya for Indian M95[3]

There is a clear distinction of Indian Munda and Southeast Asian (SEA) Mon-Khmer speakers. The predominate SEA O clades are O3 and O1a. If SEA males had carried the y-chromosome O haplogroup to India there should be evidence of these clades among the Munda speakers—but they are nil[8]. On the otherhand, SEA males carry Indian y-chromosomes such as F,H, K2 (T) and etc[8].

This indicates an early migration of Munda speakers to SEA. It suggest that Munda spread mtDNA R7 and y-chromosome haplogroup O to SEA.

Many Indians carry Munda haplogroups. The spread of Munda haplogroups are probably the result of conquest and intermarriage. The mythology of some Indian populations support this proposition.

Munda mythology claims that when they arrived in the Chotanagpur Region the Asuras would not allow Munda to stay in their territory[9]. And as a result, the Munda gods punish the Asuras by making Asura women become a part of the Munda tribe, and the Asura males were burnt to death in the Asura iron smelting furnaces[9]. This myth implies that the Munda took Asura territory after violent conflict.

A good example of this exchange comes from the Chotanagpur region. Here the Munda play an important role in the society, because they granted land to migrants who settled the Ranchi district[9]. According to the Oraon traditions they had to give up their gods and language to settle on Munda lands[9].

In conclusion , the molecular variance of the mtDNA of
Munda speakers fails to support a Southeast Asianorigin for this
population. The probable dating of y-chromosome O2a at 65kya[7]
and mtDNA R8 at 41.7 kya[13] suggest a deep rooted ancestry for
Munda speakers in India.

The presence of Munda mtDNA R7 among Dravidian and
Khasi Aslian groups is probably the result of gene flow. This view
is supported by the fact that the Dravidian speakers only arrived
in India 5kya from Africa [14-15] . This would explain why Dravidian
tribal populations and Africans share several y-chromosomes[16] .

End Notes

1. The HUGO Pan-Asian SNP Consortium. 2009. Mapping Human Genetic
Diversity in Asia. Science , 326(5959):1541 – 1545.

2. Cordaux R, Saha N, Bentley GR, Aunger R, Sirajuddin SM, et al. 2003.
Mitochondrial DNA analysis reveals diverse histories of tribal populations
from India. Eur J Hum Genet 11: 253–264.

3. Kumar V, Reddy ANS, Babu JP, et al. 2007. Y-chromosome evidence
suggests a common paternal heritage of Austro-Asiatic populations. BMC
Evolutionary Biology, 7:47.

4. Chaubey G; Metspalu M; Ying Choi; Magi R;et al. (2010). Population Genetic Structure in Indian Austroasiatic speakers: The Role of Landscape Barriers and Sex-specific Admixture .*Molecular Biology and Evolution* 2010; doi: 10.1093/molbev/msq288.
http://mbe.oxfordjournals.org/content/early/2010/10/26/molbev.msq288.full.pdf?ijkey=fq81NDB59bHykIm&keytype=ref

5.Diffloth,G. 2005. The contribution of linguistic paleontology and Austroasiatic. In Laurent Sagart, Roger Blench and Alicia Sanchez, eds., The Peopling of East Asia : Putting Together Archaeology, Linguistics and Genetics. Pp.77-80. London : Routledge Curzon.

6. Priyadarshi, P. 2010. Recent Studies in Indian Archaeo-linguistics and Archaeo-genetics having bearing on Indian Prehistory, Joint Annual Conference of Indian Archaeology Society, Indian Society for Prehistoric and Quaternary Studies, Indian History and Culture Society, Lucknow, 30 December, 2010.

7. Blench,R.2009. Reconciling reconstructions of subsistence and archaeological dates for the transition to agriculture in S.E. Asia Language Phyla.
http://www.rogerblench.info/Archaeology%20data/SE%20Asia/Siem%20Reap%202009/Blench%20Siem%20Reap%202009%20paper.pdf

8. Priyadarshi, P. 2011. Did Austro-Asiatic speakers originate in China/Southeast Asia and then migrate to India with rice agriculture. Retrieved : March 7, 2010 at
http://www.docstoc.com/docs/72779579/Review-of-Chaubey

9. Ghosh, A. 2009. Prehistory of the Chotanagpur Region Part 4: Ethnoarchaeology, Rock Art, Iron and the Asuras.Internet Journal of Biological Anthropology, vol. 3, No. 1.

10.Chandrasekar A, Kumar S, Sreenath J, Sarkar BN, Urade BP, et al. 2009 Updating Phylogeny of Mitochondrial DNA Macrohaplogroup M in India: Dispersal of Modern Human in South Asian Corridor. PLoS ONE 4(10):

e7447. doi:10.1371/journal.pone.
http://www.plosone.org/article/info:doi/10.1371/journal.pone.0007

11. Chaubey, G. 2010b. The demographic history of India: A perspective based on genetic evidence. Dissertationes Biologicae Universitatis Tartuensis. August 9 2010. Tartu University Press.

12. Chaubey G, Karnum M, Metspalu M, Deepa SR. 2008. Phylogeography of mtDNA haplogroup R7 in the Indian Peninsula. BMC Evolutionary Biology, 8:227.doi:10. 1186/1471-2148-8.227
http://www.biomedcentral.com/1471-2148/8/227

13. Thangaraj K, Nandan A, Sharma V, Sharma VK, Eaaswarkhanth M, et al. 2009 Deep Rooting In-Situ Expansion of mtDNA Haplogroup R8 in South Asia. PLoS ONE 4(8): e6545. doi:10.1371/journal.pone.
http://www.plosone.org/article/citationList.action;jsessionid=802A19AA121DB2768046A726529EAFF6.ambra01?articleURI=info%3Adoi%2F10.1371%2Fjournal.pone.0006545

14. Winters, C.2007. Did the Dravidian Speakers Originate in Africa? BioEssays, 27(5): 497-498.

15. Winters, C. 2008. ARE DRAVIDIANS OF AFRICAN ORIGIN
http://www.krepublishers.com/02-Journals/IJHG/IJHG-08-0-000-000-2008-Web/IJHG-08-4-317-368-2008-Abst-PDF/IJHG-08-4-325-08-362-Winder-C/IJHG-08-4-325-08-362-Winder-C-Tt.pdf

16. Winters, C. (2010). **Y-Chromosome evidence of an African origin of Dravidian Agriculture** International Journal of Genetics and Molecular Biology, 2(3): 030 – 033.
http://www.academicjournals.org/IJGMB/PDF/pdf2010/Mar/Winters.pdf

CHAPTER 10: BLACKS OF ANCIENT CHINA

The first group of Humans to occupy southern Africa and Asia were the Australoids. In proto-historic times these folks occupied all of Asia up into Siberia. The Australoid people probably originated in southern Africa. The Mongoloids evolved from these ancient Australoid folk around 10,000 to 15,000 BC.

From here during the numerous ice ages which affected the sea levels in the Indian Ocean, Australoids migrated across a sunken land masses which connected Africa and several points in Asia sometime before 3000 BC. From Asia they migrated into America.

Before the last Ice Age the original Australoid people were sedentary agriculturalist, due to a loss of fertile land because of increased cold and glaciation they became nomadic Mongoloids. As Asia became warmer, beginning around 4000 BC the Mongoloid groups began to move southward conquering or absorbing many Australoid elements as they moved.

By the Holocene modern Africoid groups began to enter West Asia and the Far East. The proto-type of the modern yellow races was called Chancelade man. Skeletons of this type of humans resemble those of modern Eskimos. The ancestors of the modern West Asians, and Semitic speakers are believed to be the result of the mixing of Blacks and Europeans races in ancient times.

CIVILIZATION IN CHINA CAME FROM IRAN AND THE INDUS VALLEY. The Kushites speaking Manding and Dravidian peoples introduced red-and-black pottery,wheat and millet cultivation; cattle, sheep, goats and pigs; and flexed burial with accompanying funerary furniture.

The Chinese oracle bone form of writing has affinities to Proto-Saharan scripts and pottery marks such as the Manding scripts, Harappan , Proto-Elamite and Minoan writing systems. Other evidence in China of diffusion include 1) horse, 2) spoked wheel chariot,3) bronze implements and 4)metullurgy.

To reach China the Dravidians and Manding migrated through the pass between the Tien Shan and Altai mountains following the grassy steppes that surround the desert region. The archaeological evidence proves that a sedentary tradition spread from Iran to the Altai. These diffusionary items include not only those discussed above but also weights found in China that parallel those made by the Harappans.

There is archaeological evidence indicating that farming communities placed along the route to China were of similar inspiration and date back to 3500 BC. This agricultural economy spread from west to east. This migration of sedentary folk represented the early migration of the Proto-Saharans into China.

GEOGRAPHY

China is made up of mountains and hills which formerly were covered with dense jungles and woods. This encouraged intensive prehistoric settlement in China's.

The first civilization of China was the Xia Dynasty. The Xia culture was established in the **Huang He** (Yellow River) Valley. The Huang He, includes the river and its tributaries and the upper courses of several Yangtze river tributaries.

There are three distinct regions in the Huang He river Valley: in the west the loess highlands; to the east lie the alluvial plains;

and along the seacoast we find the Shandung Peninsula. Huang

He Valley is a temperate zone , characterized by an average

rainfall of 400-800 mm, hot summers and cold winters[67].

ARCHAEOLOGY

In southeast Asia and southern China, ancient skeletal

remains represented the earliest inhabitants to be Austroloids and

Negritos (pygmies). By the beginning of the Present (Holocene)

period the population in China could be differentiated and placed

into categories designating mainly Classical Mongoloids in the

north, and Oceanic/Negro races in the south[68]. Both of these

groups may have evolved out of a common Upper Pleistocene

substratum as represented by Tzu-yang (Dzuyang) and Liuzhiang

skulls. By at least 2500 BC Africoids of the Mediterranean and

West African type entered this areas by way of the Indus Valley.

[67] Kwang-chih Chang, The archareology of ancient China, (New Haven,1977
[68] Kwang-chih Chang, "Prehistoric and early historic culture horizons and traditions in South China", Current Anthropology, 5 (1964) pp.359-375 :375

The skeletal evidence from Shandung and Giangsu China show the modern Africoid type especially at the initial Qingliengeng Machiapang phases[69].

The archaeology of southern China is related to the southeast Asian pattern, with numerous finds of chipped stone of the type found in Sezhewan, Guangxi, Yunnan and in the western part of Kwangtung as far as the Pearl River delta.

The Neolithic culture of southern China as the people parallel southeast Asian developments. There were several major centers of Neolithic culture in China where pottery and agriculture flourished. In southern China the most well known early Chinese culture was called Dapenkeng culture of the southeastern coast dating to the 5th millennium BC.

The Dapenkeng sites are characterized by cord-marked pottery. The color of the pottery dating to 4450 BC ranges from buff to dark brown. These folks had large jars and bowls and dugout canoes. Blacks also founded the Yangshao site at Huang He basin in North China.

---

[69] K.C. Chang, The archaeology of ancient China, p.76

There was an extensive mound culture in China stretching from its plateau in the west to the western coast of the Pacific, it includes Huang He and the Huai He plain of north China and the lower Valley of the Yangtze He (river) of Central China.

In accordance with the oral traditions of China, the founders of Chinese civilization were Huangdi and Fu Xi. These legendary rulers like Dai Hao, were all buried in *"zhiu"* (mounds).

The Chinese mound culture began around 3000 BC a 1000 years after a similar culture had developed in Africa. The most important Chinese mound culture is the Hu Shu site. The Hu Shu mounds were man made knolls called "terraced sites". These mounds served as l) burial places; 2) religious centers, and 3) habitation sites . These mound may have been built by the ancestors of the Oceanic people.

SOUTH CHINA

In the southeastern section of China the people at Hupeh and Guangxi made use of artificial irrigation and terracing the mountain slopes. The people probably spoke Autronesian languages and used bronze tools.

As in other Black societies the woman's role was a high one. Women also participated in the religious ceremonies. The worship of these religions consisted of a mountain and a snake cult.

The neolithic technology of Blacks in South China was typified by hunting with the bow and arrow. The stone tool inventories include shoulder axes , as those found at Yaan in Sigang, and on the island of Hainan.

The ceramics are characterized by corded red ware. There was also painted pottery, black pottery, and tripod pottery which were were later duplicated in bronze. The people practiced single burials.

The pottery inscriptions show that the Southerners already had their own writing system. The writing system of the Shang and Xia Dynasties was developed in Southern China. This writing later evolved into modern Chinese writing.

The Blacks of southern China according to Dr. Sun Sheng Ling, in A Study of the Raft,Outrigger, Double and Deck Canoes of

Ancient China, the Pacific and Indian Ocean, spoke Austronesian languages like the aborigines of Hainan and Taiwan , where Dapenkeng sites have been discovered. The contemporary people living on Taiwan claim the first inhabitants were pygmies.

The proto-Austronesian people descended from the Yuanshan culture. There were also Austronesians in northern China.

The Proto-Oceanic people which lived in southern China, invaded north China which was also inhabited by Australoids and a smallest negroid-mongoloid group. Although the Australoids had been the first inhabitants of China, by 5000 BC many of them had been exterminated or absorbed by the taller heavier Mongoloid Bak tribes, that were slowly expanding southward from the north. The recent discovery of the Loulan mummy lady of Xianjiang province dating to 4,470 years ago show that Australoid people were still occupying northern China by 4000 BC.

NORTH CHINA

North China was occupied by Australoid and small bushmanoid

Blacks until 3000 BC. The ancestors of the Oceanic Blacks were

probably Kushites.

In northern China the Blacks founded many civilizations. The

three major empires of China were the Xia Dynasty (2205-1766

BC), Shang/Yin Dynasty (1700-1050 BC) and the Zhou Dynasty.

The Zhou Dynasty was the first dynasty founded by the

Mongoloid people in China called Hua .

The founders of Xia and Shang came from the Proto-Sahara

by way of Iran. According to Chinese legends the first man Pan

Gu, used a hammer 18,000 years ago to make man.

The Chinese legends designate various heroes as the

inventors of various aspects of Chinese civilization. The Chinese

term for emperor is *Di*. Huang Di (Yellow Emperor), is the

Chinese culture hero credited with introducing boats, carts, the

bow and arrow, ceramics, wooded houses and writing.

The culture hero Huang Di is a direct link to Africa. His name

is pronounced YuHai Huangdi or Hu Nak Kunte. He was suppose

to have arrived in China from the west in 2282 BC, and settled along the banks of the Loh river in Shanxi. This transliteration of Huangdi, to **Hu Nak Kunte** is interesting because Kunte, is a common clan name among the Manding speakers[70].

In addition to Huang Di, there were three great sages who helped develop Chinese civilization. The three sages were Yao, Shun and Yu. They ruled a confederation of city-states situated on the highlands along the Huang He in north China.

Chinese civilization began along the Yellow (Huang) River (He). Here the soil was fertile and Chinese farmers grew millet 4000 years ago, later soybeans. They also raised pigs and cattle. By 3500 BC the Proto-Saharans in China were raising silkworms and making silk.

XIA

The first dynasty of China was Xia (She-ya). The Xia dynasty lasted from 2205 to 1766 BC .

Archaeologists believe that the major Xia sites are located in Shanxi and Henan. According to Chang northern Henan towards

---

[70] Clyde Winters, Blacks in China. In Survey of African Music, (Ed.) K.E. Hester (Cognella:San Diego,2010),pp.179-185.

the end of the Longshan period was the eastern part of the Xia culture[71].

Xia was probably situated in the Yihe and Luohe river valleys,and along the Yinghe and Ruhe rivers. The capital of Xia was located in the Sangshan mountains.

The origins of Xia go back to the Longshan period. During the Longshan period burial goods include a large number of weapons, including stone lanceheads and arrows. This suggest that intersocial conflict was at its height during the Longshan period, and warfare may have played a role in the raise of Xia. The Longshanoid neolithic is characterized by wheel-made pottery, bronze working, ceramics, wheeled vehicles, writing , rich grave and furnishings.

Today archaeologists believe that the Erlitou culture is the Xia Dynasty. This is supported by the fact that the historical text place Xia in Henan and southern Shanxi, the main areas for

[71] Winters,Clyde Ahmad, "The Far Eastern Origin of the Tamils", Journal of Tamil Studies , no27 (June 1985c), pages 65-92.

Erlitou.They have suggested that Henan Longshan culture and the Erlitou I-III periods are representative of the Xia Dynasty.

The artifacts of Erlitou include red,black and buff wares. Artifacts recovered from Erlitou made of stone, shell and bronze relate to the instruments recorded by Yuan Kang, in the "Yueh zhueh shu", that: "In the age of Yu, weapons were made of bronze,for building canals...and houses...."

The Proto-Saharans used a common black and red pottery that has been found from Nubia in Africa, to China. This pottery was used by the Kushites and have been found at Yangshao sites in Henan and Gansu provinces of China.

This pottery corresponds to the painted pottery used in Turkistan. Han Fei Tzu writing in the 3rd century BC, in his "**Shih Guo**", observed that:"Yu made ritual vessels painting the interior in black and the exterior in red".

The textual history of the Xia is synthesized in the **"Shih Zhi"**. This evidence was used by Hsu Husheng, of the Chinese Institute of Archaeology to find the ruins (***xu***) of Xia (Xia xu). Using these sources Hsu, was able to hypothesize that the center for traditional Xia dynasty towns was the Loyang plains and the Dengfeng and Fenhe river valley. This coincides with the Erlitou sites of this area which date to 2100-1800 BC.

Xia the first SANDAI (Three Dynasties) of ancient China. The Xia people were recognized by the Chinese as westerners, because they settled the middle Huang He. As a result they were called the Hua Xia "the middle states. A Zhou saying observed that:"The rituals [or rules of] the Three Dynasties [Sandai] are one"[72] ."

The early Xia lived on mounds, in houses made of grass and mud. Pounded earth walls surrounded villages to protect the inhabitants from attack.

The Xia spoke Dravidian and Manding languages. The major clan of the Xia was the dragon. The first clans of China were totemic. Other Xia clans include the tortoise, turtle and fish clans. The "**ZU** (TSU)" or clan was the basic point of social organization.

---

[72]Winters,Clyde Ahmad, "Blacks in Ancient China,Part 1:The Founders of Xia and Shang", Journal of Black Studies 1,no2 (1983c).

In ancient China the dragon was regarded as the deified serpent. It also denoted the symbol of perfect man, the son of Heaven, the Emperor.

The clan emblem for the Manding was the lizard. A dragon is nothing more than a giant lizard. This dragon motif was also found in Iran and Babylonian Assyrian civilization and the Anau civilization in Russia, which had similar painted pottery to the pottery styles of Henan (Xia).

The Xia built their settlements near rivers, lakes and streams. They are mentioned in the Oracle bone writing. The sacre tree of the Xia was the pine. The Xia naming system was the same as that used by the Shang.

The founder of the Xia Dynasty was Yu. His father was Gun. Myths about Gun are found throughout southwest Shanxi. Yu's son founded the Pa culture.

The Pa culture was a megalithic culture. Great Yu was the regulator of the waters and builder of canals. He invented wetfield agriculture.

Yu was born in Shihnew. His mother was Sewge (Seuge). She is alleged to have become pregnant and swallowed a spirit's pearl.

Under the orders of Emperor Shun, Yu was to dredge the Yellow River. Yu traveled the empire for 10 years draining the land of water. One tradition claims that "but for Yu we should all have been fishes".

Beginning with Xia the fundamental political unit of this dynasty and succeeding dynasties of China was the "YI" or walled town. These yi, were organized into small and large **"GUO"** (states). Each **guo**, was known as a "**SHIH**".

The rulers of the **guo**, were members of an agnati clan or "**XING**". The **xing**, ruled over members of their own clan and non-related clans living in the various **yi**, forming the **guo**.

Emperor Shun, appears to have given Egeu, his son, the principality of Shang, and Yu the principality of Xia. After the death of Shun, Yu became the leader of the confederation of Seihshin, Xia and Shang. According to Gu Tsu Yu, in the "**Du**

Shih fang yu Zihiyao", written in the 1600's: "It is traditionally stated that when Yu assembled the lords at Dushan there were ten thousand states [cities] that came carrying jades and silks".

The first ancestor of the Xia , was Qi, the son of Di (Emperor) Yu. The Xia Dynasty remained strong until a tyrant Zhieh came to power. In 1766 BC, Zhieh was deposed and exiled by Zheng Dang, ruler of Shang.

The first capital of Xia was Yangcheng. This city was in southwestern Shanxi. Archaeologist believe that Taosi and Wangchenggang may be Xia cities[73].

Taosi, dates to 2500 to 1900 BC. Here the people raised oxen,pigs and sheep. They grew millet. Their homes were built half-way below ground.

They smelted copper. The coiled dragon motif is common at this site along with crocodile skin drums.

---

[73] An Jinhuai, "In Search of China's Oldest Capital", China Pictorial, (1986) pages 39-41

The Taosi site is important because the artifacts excavated from the more than 1,000 tombs, indicate that a hereditary system of chiefs was already established and class distinctions.

The dragon motif at Taosi, may have been the totem of the Xia dynasts at Taosi. This would correspond to Chinese legends of the Long (Dragon)tribe, Huan Long (Dragon Breeding clan) and Yu Long (Defend the Dragon) clan. The dragon legends are associated with the Chinese sages Yan, Yao, Shun and Yu.

The capital of Xia Yangcheng, is believed to be the city of Wangshenggang. As mentioned earlier the yi, or walled city was the basic political unit of Xia. These walls were built layer upon layer and called "Hangtu", Chinese traditions allege that Yu's father Gun built the first hangtu.

Wangshenggang site is 10,000 sq. meters near the Wudu river. This structure contains skeletons of all ages, ceramics, sickles and shell tools.

SHANG DYNASTY

The decline of the Xia empire led to the rise of Shang as the leading state in the confederation. The clan totem of Shang, was the bird. In the "Yen sen Zhi", it is written that the mother of Xieh, the founder of Shang-Yin, was impregnated by a Black of Xia: "Three persons including Zhien Di went to take a bath. They saw that a black bird dropped an egg. Zhien Di took and devoured it, became impregnated and gave birth to Xieh. Xieh grew up assisted Yu, in his work to control the flood with success".

According to the Shang poem "Hsuan Niao", "Heaven bode the dark bird/to come down and bear Shang". All of these quotes relate to the African origin of the Shang rulers. Many of the Shang spoke a Dravidian language.

The founders of Shang are often called "*YI*". Yi, means "Great Bowman". The symbol for Yi, in Chinese is translated Dagung. This character has two parts "*DA*" 'great', and "*GUNG*" 'a bow'. The Name Yi, and similarity in the name Kuishuang (Kushana) and Kashshu highlight the archaeological evidence pointing to a western origin for many elements of Chinese civilization. The bird totem of Shang suggest that the Shang were predominately Dravidian speakers.

The Shang culture was founded by the Kushites thus the name Yi 'Great Bowman', this corresponds to Steu, the name for the founders of Ta-Seti.

The Yi seem to have lived in both north and south China. Fu Ssu-nien,in "*Yi Hsis Tunghsi Shuo*", makes it clear that the Shang culture bearers remained allied to the rest of the Yi people who lived in southern China.

The founders of Xia are usually referred to as Yueh as opposed to Yi.

It would appear that the Yi (Dravidian speakers) and Yueh (Manding speakers) came to China by land and sea.

The earliest Shang capital was established at Zhengzhou. There were 30 kings of Shang, the last 14 reigned at Anyang, Henan in the Yellow River Valley. The Anyang Shang were classical mongoloids not Yueh people.

Artefacts discovered at Panglongzheng, Hubei far to the south in the Yangtze River Valley show bronze vessels 'culturally homogeneous' to Zengzhou in every respect. At this time China's environment was different.

China was much wetter and warmer several millennium before the Christian era. Many animals found only in southeast Asia and southern China today lived in the north. In Anyang area during the Shang period there were two harvests of millet and rice. There were also elephants and rhinoceros in the area according to the oracle bone records.

During the Shang period the Yi wrote much information on bones and turtle shells. This form of writing is called oracle bone writing.

The plants cultivated by the Shang had first been domesticated by the Yi and Yueh people in south China and later taken northward as they colonized northern China.

Shang society was based on totemic clans called "*ZU*". The clan signs are visible in clan emblems in bronze and oracle bone inscriptions, they were based on animal signs. The symbol of the

Shang was the BIRD. Later Shang clans, probably represented the nomadic Proto-Saharans that settled China that came from Iran with their cattle.

In the southern world, due to a sedentary economy, such concepts as matriarchy, monotheistic religion and totemism were the major aspects of social organization. In examining the history of Blacks in ancient China we find that totemic names denoting blackness refers to Black creators of Shang, as opposed to the Mongoloid founders of Zhou Dynasty, e.g., "li min" 'the black heads" or " Xi Qiang" 'the black Qiang".

The first Shang king was **Xuan Wang** 'Dark King' (**Xuan** means black, **Wang** means King).The founder of the Shang Dynasty was called **Xuan Niao** "Black Bird", another Shang king was called **Xuan Mu** "Black Oxen". The first ruler of Shang is often referred to as **Xuan Di** "Black Emperor".

The Shang kingdom flourished in the Huang He basin in the Henan province after 1766 BC. The Shang-Yin cultivated rice, millet and wheat.
They used many metals including copper and tin.

Each Shang town had its own king. The nobles ruling the Shang cities recognized the Shang Di (Shang Emperor) as the head of the confederation because his powers were considered to be ordained by Heaven or God.

Written history begins in China with the Shang Dynasty (1500 - 1027). The ruler of Shang was recognized as both the military and religious leader. As a high priest the Shang Di, made sacrifice and paid homage to the gods for the nation and the people.

The source of Shang history are references to this dynasty in ancient Chinese books, archaeology and the oracle bone inscriptions. After heating these bones, the priests would interpret the cracks and answer questions on various subjects relating to everyday life. Other Shang records were kept on tablets of wood and bamboo.

The Shang are best known for their work in bronze. Shang artists made fine pottery and bronze vases of different shapes, often standing on three legs. The bronze works, along with work of art made from ivory and jade illustrate the high level of Shang technology.

In 1027 BC, the Shang were conquered by nomads who invaded the region from the Northwest.

According to the "Yin pen Chi", the founding ancestor of Shang was Xieh a member of the Tzu clan. His mother was Zhien Ti, who according to Chinese myth was impregnated by the "black bird" Yu[74].

The use of the "black bird", as Yu , the father of Xieh relates to a totem popular among the Black tribes of ancient China. This passage indicates that the founders of Shang were of mixed origin. The fact that the bird myths such as the one above are mainly centered on the east coast also suggest a Black origin for Shang since this area was the heartland of ancient Black China.

The eastern coast was a major area of Black Habitation in ancient times. One of the popular symbols of the southern Chinese tribes was the egret bird, according to F. Hirth, in "*The ancient History of China*".

---

[74] Allan, S , "Sons of Suns:Myth and Totemism in Early China", Bulletin of the School of Oriental and African Studies (BSOAS) XLIV,(1981) pages 290-326; and Allan, S , "Drought, Human Sacrifice and the Mandate of Heaven in a Lost Text from the Shang Shu", BSOAS XLVII, (1984) pages 523-535; and

This view is also supported by many archaeologist including K.C. Chang, evidence which indicates that the neolithic Mongoloid population of north China resembled the Oceanic-mongoloid type, not the modern Mongoloid group we find living in China and much of southeast Asia today.

The name Shang refers to a town which was the early capital of the empire. According to the Shang poem Xuan Niao: "Heaven bade the dark bird / to come down and bear the Shang".

But during the last 273 years of Shang dynasty, Shang was not the capital of the empire. By this time Classical Mongoloid people had conquered the Dravidian speaking Shang. This view is supported by the Zhou poem "*Pi Kung*", which talks about the Great King "who lived on the southern slopes of mount Qi/and began to trim Shang".

The Shang had extensive trade relations with the Southerners. The sources of Shang copper and tin were in the southern areas of China. Here the southerners mined metals and sold them to Shang.

The monetary system of the Shang included the use of cowrie shells. The cowrie shells appear to have been introduced into northern China from the eastern seacoast.

For divination the Yi of Shang used turtle shells. The characters written on the shells give us the earliest written records of China's first civilization.

Both the ancient Chinese and Africans had similar naming practices. As in Africa the Shang child had a name. The Shang child was named according to the days of the "ZUN", on which he was born. There were ten days in each in each zun. These days are called the ten celestrial signs.

TEN CELESTIAL SIGNS
CHIA YI PING TING WU CHI KENG HSIN JEN KULI

Shang was destroyed by nomads. These people came from central Asia, some of these people may have been Tibetans. Due to nomadic invasions the Shang empire, the Yin had to constantly move their capitals around until they were conquered by the Zhou.

THE QIANG/KUSHANA

The Qiang may be the ancestors of the Kushana. The Kushana were called Yuehchih by the Chinese. The Chinese literature says the the Kushana originally came from Gansu province. They were also called the Kuishuang. They originally came from the West (Iran) .

The early inhabitants of Gansu, used the black-and-red ware common to Proto-Saharan civilization. Gansu is the epicenter for the spread of the Kushana into Central Asia.

The Qijia culture had black-and-red ware. Qijia culture is in Gansu,it dates 2500 to 1500 BC[75].

---

[75] Winters, Clyde Ahmad, "The Dravido Harappan Colonization of Central Asia", Central Asiatic Journal 34, no1-2 (1990), pages 120-144.

Qijia was related to Longshan culture of the east and represent a "different ethnic strain" probably of a distinctive cultural tradition.

The Qijia culture is characterized by domesticated cattle, sheep and pig. This was the most advanced agro-pastoral group in early China. These farmers grew millet. In addition, the pottery signs correspond to Proto- Saharan signs.

Here we see the same marine migration pattern of the Proto-Saharans. The area of distribution of Qijia was along the upper Weishui Valley in the east, the Huangshui valley of Qinghai in the west, Ningxia and westernmost Inner Mongolia in the north. The distribution of Qijia sites corresponds to areas where the Altaic languages were originally spoken.

The Qijia culture extended into West Yunnan. In the flat mountain areas there were farming communities and domesticated animals. These farmers used the hoe to cultivate their crops. Their domesticated animals include ox,horse , sheep, chicken and dog.

The West Yunnan culture share elements of the early Gansu culture. Excavated burials from West Yunnan has yielded many figurines of domesticated animals. In addition pig and sheep mandibles have been found in many burials.

The Qiang were often called "*Li Qiang*" 'Black Qiang". This ethnic group migrated from the Gansu-Qinghai Highlands to Northwest Yunnan. The Qiang were part of the Yueh clan.

Qiang were farmers. During the Anyang-Shang period the Qiang were made into slaves . The Anyang-Shang were classical mongoloids, they made the Qiang their agricultural workers and artisans.

THE NEGRITOS/PYGMIES

Many of the Qiang migrated into Yunnan. Yunan was a center of Anu or negrito civilization.

The Zhou conquered many negrito nations. These Anu were called "*MAN*", and "**KUNLUNG**". Many of these Blacks still live in Cochin China and Yunnan.

The Chinese first came in contact with the negritos in 2116

BC,they are mentioned in the **"Zhou Li"**, as living along the

Yellow River. The **Man** tribe, of the Yangtze River basin area were

also constantly at war with the Zhou.

The **Man**, were closely related to the Tibetans of Szechuan. The

Man states were ruled by princes. These states were organized

into a confederation.

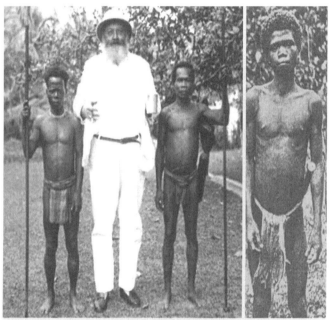

The Semang - one of the original people of the Malay peninsular

The negritos occupied much of Szechuan, Yunnan and Kaehun in the southeast, to Yunchang in the southwest. Many of the Anu were forced into the Malay Peninsula by the advance of various mongoloid Chinese tribes toward the coast after 200 BC.

Chapter 11: OCEANIA

Most of the inhabitants of Oceania are Africoids. They made their way eastward from Africa through India, to Southeast Asia, southern China,Indonesia and the Islands in the Pacific.

A simple observation of Melanesians and Aborigines make it clear that they resemble Africans moreso than Aborigines--the original settlers of Asia.

Current physical anthropological research makes it clear there are craniometric difference between Australoids /Australians representatives of the OOA population, Mongoloids and Melanoids; craniometric differences that indicate two migrations of the Black Variety into the Pacific and East Asia.

Tsuenehiko Hanihare discussed the phenotypic variations between these populations(1). Tsuenehiko classified these people into three major populations Southeast Asian Mongoloids (Polynesians), the Australians or Austroloid type and the Nicobar and Andaman (Melanoid) samples which he found lie between the

predominately Southeast Asian and Australoid/Australian type [76].

The Australian aborigines and Melanesians show cranonical

variates and represent two distinct Black populations[77]. The

Australoids or Australians live mainly in Australia and the

highland regions of Oceania, the Melanoid people on the

otherhand live in the coastal regions of Near Oceania and Fiji. D.J

de Laubenfels discussed the variety of Blacks found in Asia.

Laubenfiels explained that Negroids/Melanoids such as the

Tasmanians are characterized by wooly black hair and sparse

body hair [78]. Australoids or Australians on the otherhand have

curly, wavy or straight hair and abundant body hair. Other

differences between these Black populations include Negroid /

Melanoid brows being vertical and without eyebrow ridges,

whereas Australoid brows are sloping and with prominent

---

[76]Tsunehiko Hanihare, Interpretation of craniofacial variations and diversification of East and Southeast Asia. In Bioarchaeology of Southeast Asia. (Eds.) Marc Oxenhan and Nancy Tayles (pp.91-111). Cambridge, 2005.

[77] . D.J. Laubenfels, Australoids, Negroids and Negroes: A suggested explanation for their distinct distributions. Annals Association of Am. Geographers, 58(1), 1968: 42-50.

[78] Ibid., p.44.

ridges[79].

This led M. Pietrusewky to recognize two separate

colonizations of the Pacific by morphologically distinct populations

one Polynesian and the other Melanesian[80]. Pietrusewky's

research indicates a clear separation between the Australian-

Melanesian crania and the Polynesian crania. The findings indicate

an origin for the Polynesians in Southeast Asia, and an early

Australo-Melanesian presence in East Asia[81] .

Laubenfels argues that the Australians are remnants of the

original African migration to the region 60kya. This view is

supported by David Bulbeck who found that the Australian

craniometrics are different from the Mongoloid (Polynesian), and

Melanoid crania metrics[82] . This research indicates that whereas

---

[79] Ibid., p.43-44.
[80] Michael Pietrusewky, A multivariate craniometric study of the prehistoric and modern inhabitants of Southeast Asia, East Asia and surrounding regions:A human kaleidoscope. Cambridge Studies in Biological and Evolutionary Anthropology, No. 43, 2006: 59-90.

[81] David Bulbeck, Australian Aboriginal craniometrics as construed through FORDISC, 2005. Retrieved: 4/2/2008: http://arts.anu.edu.au/bullda/oz_craniometrics.html ; and M. Pietrusewsky, The Physical anthropology of the Pacific, East Asia: A multivariate craniometric analysis. . In L. Sagart, R. Blench, A. Sanchez-Mazos (Eds), The peopling of East Asia Putting together Archaeology,Linguistics and Genetics (pp.201-229). RutledgeCurzon, 2005.

[82] David Bulbeck, Australian Aboriginal craniometrics as construed through FORDISC, 2005. Retrieved: 4/2/2008: http://arts.anu.edu.au/bullda/oz_craniometrics.html

Australian aborigine crania agree with the archaic population of

Asia and first group of Africans to exit Africa, they fail to

correspond to the Sahulland crania which are distinctly of

Southwest Pacific or Melanoid affinity. This suggests that by the

rise of Sahulland there were two distinct Black populations in Asia

one Austroloid and the other Melanoid [83].

The Melanesian type does not appear in East Asia (Siberia)

until after 5000 BC. This is thousands of years after Luizia and

Eva Neharon had existed in Brazil and Mexico respectively.

By the Neolithic the Melanoids or Papuans are associated with

millet cultivation at Yangshao and Lougshan according to

Pietrusewky's work [84]. Tsang argues that the probable homeland

of the Austronesian speakers was the Pearl River delta, here the

Melanoid people cultivated millet [85]. Sagart believes that there is

a Proto-Sino-Tibetan-Austronesian family of languages based on

[83] Ibid., passim.
[84] and M. Pietrusewsky, The Physical anthropology of the Pacific, East Asia: A multivariate craniometric analysis. . In L. Sagart, R. Blench, A. Sanchez-Mazos (Eds), The peopling of East Asia Putting together Archaeology,Linguistics and Genetics (pp.201-229). RutledgeCurzon, 2005.
[85] Tsang Cheng-Hwa, Recent discoveries at Tapenkeng culture sites in Taiwan;Implications for the problem of Austronesian origins. In The peopling of East Asia Putting together Archaeology, Linguistics and Genetics ,(Eds) L. Sagart, R. Blench, A. Sanchez-Mazos (pp.63-74). RutledgeCurzon, 2005.

the millet culture the Melanoids introduced to China [86].

The craniometrics make it clear the ancient Americans are not related to the Melanesians.

The ancestors of the Melanesians and Polynesians probably lived in East Asia. The late appearance of Melanoid people from East Asia on the shore areas of Oceania would explain the differences between the genetic make up of Melanesians living in the highlands and Melanesians living along the shore[87].

The skeletal evidence from East Asia suggests that the most recent common ancestor (TMRCA) of the Polynesians and some of the coastal Melanesians may be mainland East Asia, not Taiwan[88]. The ancestral population for the shoreline Melanesians was

[86] L. Sagart, Sino-Tibetan-Austronesian an Updated and improved argument. In L. Sagart, R. Blench, A. Sanchez-Mazos (Eds), The peopling of East Asia Putting together Archaeology, Linguistics and Genetics (pp.161-176). RutledgeCurzon, 2005.

[87] . Manfred Kayser, Oscar Lao, Kathrin Saar, Silke Brauer, Xingyu Wang, Peter Nürnberg, Ronald J. Trent, Mark Stoneking Genome-wide Analysis Indicates More Asian than Melanesian Ancestry of Polynesians. The American Journal of Human Genetics - 10 January 2008, 82 (1); pp. 194-198 ; and J. S. Fredlaender, F.R. Friedlaender, J.A. Hodgson, M. Stoltz, G. Koki, G. Horvat,S. Zhadanov, T. G. Schurr and D.A. Merriwether, Melanesian mtDNA complexity, PLoS ONE, 2(2) 2007: e248.

[88] F. Weidenreich F., Bull. Nat. Hist. Soc. Peiping 13, (1938-40): p. 163; Kwang-chih Chang, Archaeology of ancient China (Yale University Press, 1986) p. 64; 5. G. H. R. von Koenigswald, A giant fossil hominoid from the pleistocene of Southern China, Anthropology Pap. Am Museum of Natural History, no.43, 1952, pp. 301-309) ; K. C. Chang, The archaeology of ancient China, (Yale University Press: New Haven, 1977): p. 76; and Winters, Clyde Ahmad, "The Far Eastern Origin of the Tamils", Journal of Tamil Studies, no27 (June 1985), pp. 65-92.

probably forced from East Asia by Proto-Polynesians as they were

pushed into Southeast Asia by the Han or contemporary Chinese.

This would explain the genetic diversity existing among shoreline

Melanesians, in comparison to the genetic homogeneity among

isolated inland Melanesian, like the Highland New Guineans.

There were two Shang Dynasties, one Melanoid (Qiang-

Shang) and the other Proto-Polynesian (Yin-Shang). The first

Shang Dynasty was founded by Proto-Melanesians or Melanoids

belonging to the Yueh tribe called Qiang [89]. The Qiang lived in

Qiangfeng, a country to the west of Yin-Shang, Shensi and

Yunnan.

The archaeological evidence also indicates that the

Polynesians probably originated in East Asia [90]. Consequently, the

Polynesian migration probably began in East Asia, not Southeast

Asia. Taiwan genetically probably belongs to the early Polynesians

---

[89] Winters, Clyde Ahmad, "The Far Eastern Origin of the Tamils", Journal of Tamil Studies, no27 (June 1985), pp. 65-92.

[90]. S. S. Ling, A study of the Raft, Outrigger, Double, and Deck canoes of ancient China, the Pacific, and the Indian Ocean. The Institute of Ethnology Academic Sinica. Nankang, Taipei Taiwan, 1970; Kwang-chih Chang, "Prehistoric and early historic culture horizons and traditions in South China", Current Anthropology, 5 (1964): pp. 359-375: 375); and Winters,Clyde Ahmad, "Dravidian Settlements in ancient Polynesia", India Past and Present 3, no2 (1986): pp. 225-241.

who settled Taiwan before they expanded into outer Oceania.

Given the archaeological record of intimate contact between Proto-Polynesians and Proto-Melanoids, neither a "slow boat" or "express train" explains the genetic relationship between the Melanesian and Polynesian populations. This record makes it clear that these populations lived in intimate contact for thousands of years and during this extended period of interactions both groups probably exchanged genes.

There were probably four major migration of the Africans into the Pacific. The first migration was the migration of early homo sapiens sapiens out of Africa around 60,000 BC. The remnants of this migration is probably the highland Melanesians and Australians. These people demonstrate the physical type associated with the early homo sapien sapiens.

The second migration was a migration of pgymy and bushman type people around 20,000-15,000 BC. These people settle many Indian Ocean Islands, India, and East Asia. Remnants of these people are the Munda speakers of India and inhabitants of the

Nicobar and Andamen islands. These people made little impact in Oceania which was predominantely still occupied at this time by the Australian type people.

Andaman People

Munda People

Bushman

The third migration was of modern Africans. This migration

occurned between 2000-1500 BC. These people spoke languages related to the Niger-Congo and Dravidian groups. They are predominately known as Kushites and spread the use of red-and-black pottery, cattle rearing and millet and yam cultivation to India, Central and East Asia .These Africans also spread a common megalithic culture from Africa to Hawaii. The Fijians were probably part of this group.

The fourth migration took place between 1000-500 BC. This migration resulted from the Hua (contemporary) Chinese defeating the Yin-Shang situated at Anyang, China. These Africans forced out of East Asia and Southeast Asia settle the low land areas of Near Oceania. The lapita artifacts suggest that some of these Africans may have also made their way to Fiji.

The Hua defeat of the Yin-Shang forced Africans and Dravidians out of North China into Central Asia, and onto the Pacific islands. Dravidian speakers (mainly Tamil) were forced into Central Asia, and via Yunnan Province across Southeast Asia and into South India.

Although most Yin people remained in Indonesia. Other Yin

people, or Proto-Polynesians began to settle the Pacific Islands during this period.

Polynesians or Oceanic-Africoids practiced artificial irrigation,megalithic architecture, well developed religion and divine kingship. Matrilineal descent was part of Pacific societies.

The people in this area practiced the Lapita culture. These folk were longdistance merchants. They were mobile colonists who communicated by sea.

The names for the Pacific Islands relate to the people who lived on the Islands. For example, Melenesia, means "Black Islands"; Micronesia, means "Small Islands"; and Polynesian , means "Many Islands".

The earliest culture of the Pacific was the Lapita culture. It spread in the Pacific area between 1600-1200 BC. The Lapita culture is characterized by ceramic cooking pots, bowls and dishes. The ceramics are laced with intricate horizontal bands and geometric designs. The motifs on the ceramics agree with Polynesian tattoo signs.

The Lapita people ate seafood. They also collected nuts and fruits. These folk also had domesticated animals including pigs and chickens.

The Lapita people were part of the megalithic culture element which invaded the Australoid area directly from Africa.

The Oceanic Africoids or Melanesians were expert seamen. Lapita culture was early established in the area of the Bismark Archipelago. From here bearers of Lapita culture went to colonize Tonga and Somoa.

They used the stars to navigate the Pacific. There was an extensive net-work of trade routes extending over 2,700 km.

Yueh tribesmen from southern China began to settle in the Pacific after 500 BC these people spoke Dravidian and African languages. Yueh inspired the Dong-Son culture. Between A.D. 200 to 700 classical Mongoloids began to dominate Eastern Polynesian Islands. These mongoloids are called Yi, in Chinese literature , but they should not be confused with the Yi of Shang.

Through a process of slow infiltration by 1200 BC a smallest Africoid- mongoloid race, was being pushed southward by the modern Mongoloid group that dominates China today.

As the mongoloid people began to occupy the Southeast Asian mainland the Afro-Dravidian populations set out by boat to settle the Polynesian islands. Many Polynesians who are classified as mongoloid people show clear genetic characteristics inherited from the Australoid peoples. By A.D. 1000 the mongoloid peoples began to mix with the Australoid and Oceanic peoples; by this time the Mongoloids were hunting Oceanic people to sell as slaves.

The peoples on the continental Pacific islands grew many crops. The chief food for these people were sweet potatoes and "taro". Their diet was supplimented by fish and pigs.

The low-island people lived almost entirely on coconut palm. Wood for houses came from the trunks. The meat of the coconut was used for food. The husks of coconuts were made into ropes and nets.

All Pacific island cultures did not decline after A.D. 1000. At the time of European arrival in the area the people were building temple mounds similar to step pyramids. They engaged in long distance trade over the Pacific and possessed their own kings.

CHAPTER 12: HISTORY OF THE PACIFIC ISLANDERS

The first population to occupy Southeast Asia and China was Homo erectus. Remains of this hominid have been found in central and eastern Java, dating to the Lower and Middle Pleistocene.

Around 55,000 to 35,000 years ago the ancestors of modern Australoids were living in Southeast Asia. The Australoid people now live in Australia.

These populations were later joined by Negritos (Anu) like the Semang.

Negrito remnants are still found in Cochin China, Malay States,Andamen Islands, Philippine Islands and Formosa.

Anus late as the beginning of the Christian era Black tribes occupied the Chinese provinces of Yunnan and Szechuan.

Austronesian refers to the language family of the modern Pacific Islanders including those of Polynesia, Micronesian, Melenesia, Indonesia, and the Philippines.

During the Pleistocene sea levels were lower and the Islands of the Pacific were connected to the mainland. This land mass was named SUNDALAND.

Until very recently, in geological time, the Southeast Asian area extended to the Indonesian Islands, the Philippines and on across New Guinea to Australia and Tasmania.

Originally these Islands were settled by Australian people. Around 12kya pygmy people began to settle these Islands.

The Chinese linguistic data suggest that the Northern Chinese show more homogeneity than the southern Chinese because it was only recently settled. This view is supported by the fact that the earlier inhabitants of the North were first Negroid/Africoid and called Naxi, Li min, Yueh, Man and Kunlun; and Classical Mongoloids called Yi and thus ethnically dissimilar to the contemporary Chinese speakers.

The physical type common to South China in the past was similar to the Oceanic peoples. The proto-type came from the Dzuyang man. The Dzuyang culture was situated in South China. Other skeletal examples of this type come from Dawenkou culture. At Dawenkou there was skull deformation and extraction of teeth--customs which are similar to the Polynesian group.

The south Chinese share religious customs and blood type with the Pacific Islanders. The bird egg motif is found along the eastern coastal region. The bird egg motif is also established among the Polynesians, whose creator god TANGAROA MAUI, had an identical birth as the founders of the Shang dynasty from a bird's egg. Moreover, the Oceanic people and South Chinese share the same blood type HLA antigen.

The classical mongoloids formed the Anyang Shang, of Second Shang Dynasty as opposed to the Li min "Black Heads", who founded both the Xia, and First Shang Dynasties. The Yi drove the Li min and Yueh people into

Western China, especially Gansu and Yunnan.

The Yi tribes, settled Polynesia after they were forced southward by first the Zhou and later Qin armies. This is supported by the similarity of the Lapita pottery, and the Dapenkeng and Longshan pottery from southern China.

The Yin-Shang Oracle term for boat BA (PA), and the Polynesia words **PAHI, PAE PAE** agree. This along with the affinity of the unique relief carving from Moanalua Valley, O'ahu Island that resemble the Yin-Shang totem sign *Fu Tzu/Fu Hao* without the Fu element all agree with a South Chinese migration to the Pacific Islands.

As the ice melted after the end of the last Ice age, the sea levels began to raise and the inhabitants of the Sunda(land) Shelf retreated to the coast of South China and northern Vietnam. Other groups such as the Negritos were stranded on many Islands as the Pacific Ocean covered up Sundaland. Pottery from the lowest levels of sites in southeast Asia is found in the Philippines. By 4000 BC, Australoid people began to leave the mainland. They settled as far as Madagascar and Easter Island.

The earliest Austronesian language speakers appear well established on the mainland by around 6000 years ago. Except for Formosa, there are no Austronesian speakers on the mainland. Some linguists see a relationship between the Austronesian and Thai languages.

The first Austronesian sites in Southeast Asia and southern China include the Qlinglingkang culture. Here 6000 years ago people made stone knives and pottery and raised cattle and pigs. Other Austronesian sites include Dapenkeng, Lungshahoid, Hoabinhian and Yuanshan. The ancient Austronesians cultivated rice, millet, yams and sugarcane.

The Austronesian speakers built the earliest sea going canoes and were great fishermen. During their spread from the mainland to the Islands, they took along tubers and fruits. Cereal plant cultivation was not taken with these sea-voyagers as they occupied the Islands in Micronesia and Polynesia.

These ancient folk made their homes atop mounds and used irrigation to grow crops. They used stone and wooden tools.

The Austronesians are also credited with inventing outrigger canoes,and even the Junk and Sampan.

As early as 9000 years ago the Austronesian speakers had developed elaborate drainage technics and they were sedentary people practicing horticulture. As early as 5000 BC metallurgy was known, iron was being exploited by Austronesians 3000 years ago.

The Austronesian pottery and horticulture appear first in Southeast Asia, the Philippines and eastern Indonesia by 5000 BC, later it spread to Melanesia.

The ancestors of the Oceanic-Africoid people appear to have been mound builders who began to expand out of Africa in search of new homes to replace the flood.Negritos whose civilization was destroyed by the great.

By 3000 BC Oceanic-Africoid people began to invade Micronesia, these Melenesian people are very closely related to the Africoid group in modern Africa in culture and language.

Southern China was a center of civilization for the Austronesian and Oceanic people. These Blacks are called Yi and Yueh in the Chinese records.

These Austronesian and Polynesians also made beautiful bronze drums which were decorated with examples of their sailing craft.

The Xia and Shang dynasties of China as illustrated earlier were created by the Blacks as was Chinese writing.

Around 4kya a megalithic culture expanded from Africa to the Islands in the Indian and Pacific Oceans. The people who carried this culture lived in Nubia. They probably belonged to the C-Group. These people were called Kushites. These Kushites mainly spoke Niger-Congo languages.

Tonga step pyramid

First, the Fijians claim they came from Africa. We know a megalithic culture expanded from Africa into the Indian/Pacific Ocean areas after 2000 BC.

Pyramid of Mauritius

Secondly, African place names are found in the Pacific and correspondences between lexical items. Common Terms:

English Manding Melanesian Polynesian

arrow bye,bya fana,pane fana,pana

Father baba babi papa

Man tye ta taga-ta

head ku tequ-qa tuku-noa

pot daga taga taga

vase bara pora,bora bora-bora

fish yege ige, ika ika

ox, cattle konga,gunga kede kuda

The ancient Austronesians cultivated rice, millet, yams and sugarcane.

It would appear that the Polynesians learned agriculture from the Manding as illustrated below:

- Polynesian English Manding

  *talun fallow, land daa

  *tanem to plant, sow daa

  *suluq torch, jet of flame suu

  *kuDen cooking pot,bowl ku

This evidence provides linguistic and anthropological support for the Fiji tradition. It is wrong that you guys deny a people history just because your European masters to do not present evidence in support of a native tradition.

Recently Williams John Page (1988) discussed the Lakato Hypothesis. The Lakato Hypothesis stated simply implies that the Melanesian people of Fiji were carried to the Pacific Islands by Indonesian maritime merchants after they had colonized parts of East and central Africa. In these Indonesian centers, Page believes that the Africans "gravitated into the Indonesian inspired trade". Page wrote that : "It is further suggested that the Lakato colonies inAfrica were the principal contributors to the earliest settlements of Malagasy and responsible for the traces of Indonesian influence in Africa which have endured into modern times, as identified by previous investigators".

To support this hypothesis Page presents place names that are made up of African ethnic names (AEN) as roots for Fijian placenames. These toponyms include a multitude of hills, streams and villages composed of a simple AEN root plus a Fijian placenames e.g.,koro, wai-ni-, vatu and na-. Page (1988, p.34) found 270 AEN's forming part of Fijian place names (FPN). The interesting fact about the AEN and FPN cognates is that they are found in West Africa and not East Africa. (Page 1988, p.47)

This fact negates Page's (1988) hypothesis because there are no rivers in Africa that link East Africa and West Africa. This suggest that Africans who later settled West Africa must have been in the Pacific long before the Austronesians arrived on Madagascar. This view is supported by the fact that the classical mongoloid people did not arrive in the Pacific area until after 500 B.C.

Page believes that the AEN-FPN cognates are the result of the establishment of Indonesian colonies first along the Zambia river and from there into Central and Western Africa between the fourth and eleventh centuries A.D. During this period Bantu speakers are believed to have been incorporated into the Indonesian Lakota culture and between the eleventh to sixteenth A.D. settled in Melanesia by Lakota fleets. (Page 1988, p.66) Although Page's theory is interesting the fact that the AENs that are FPN's are prefixed to a multitude of hills, streams and villages" indicate that these place names are very old because the names for hills and streams are rarely changed.

Page (noted four common prefixes used in the FPN's: Koro 'village,hill', wai-ni- 'water of'; vatu- 'stone'; and na- 'the'. These terms are closely related to Manding terms as illustrated below:

FPN	English	Manding
koro	hill	kuru
koro	village	so-koro
wai-ni	water of	ba-ni 'course of water'
vatu	stone	bete
na	the	ni

As illustrated above the AENs and Manding terms are analogous for 'hill', 'the' and 'of'. It would appear that the FPN /w/ corresponds to Manding /b/. Due to the thousands of miles separating the Manding and AENs, this cognate can be explained as loan words. Given the full agreement of these terms suggest a genetic relationship between AENs and Manding and descent from Paleo-African.

In addition to AENs serving as FPNs we find many toponyms in Oceania that corresponds to West African place names. Below we see 36 place names from Oceania and WestAfrica that share full correspondence. Manding ,Polynesian and Melanesian share many terms for kinship, dwellings, topographical features, dwellings and utensils.

WEST AFRICA OCEANIA
Alamand Alamanda
Alika Alika
Alika Arika
Babonga Babonga
Bagola Bagola
Batori Batori
Bakaka Bakaka
Bambula Bambula
Buduri Buduri
Burbura Burbura
Gambia Gambia

Kalobi Kalobi
Kalonda Kalonda
Kalonga Kalonga
Kamalo Kamalo
Kambia Kambia
Kamori Kamori
Kantara Kantara
Karako Karako
Kayata Kayata
Kukula Kukula
Magari Magari
Magura Maguri
Makara Makara
Marosi Maros
Oronga Oronga
Palanka Palanka
Parapara Parapara
Sio Sio
Sumbura Sumbura
Tamana Tamana
Taraba Taraba
Taramal Taramal
Teleki Teleki
Totoki Totoki
Varong Varong

See full article: http://olmec98.net/pac1.htm

A recent article on Nigerian place names in India[91]. Like Baiye,
Dr. Balakrishnan found almost 500 Nigerian placenames, and 46
tribal names in Koraput, India; and 110 ethnonyms of Koyas in
Nigeria. **This led Dr. Balakrishnan to declare that
:"However, the overwhelming evidence available from the**

---

[91] Dr. R. Balakrishnan titled "African roots of the Dravidian-speaking Tribes: A case in
Onomastics", International Journal of Dravidian Linguistics, 34(1) (2005),pp.153-202

toponymic corpuses of Koraput and Nigeria, and ethnonyms, surnames and personal names of Koyas seem more adequate to propose an African origin to the Koyas, the Dravidian speakers" (p.177)

It is interesting to note that we find Koya placenames in Nigeria, and Nigerian place names on the East Coast of India (Balakrishnan), Nigerian place names throughout the Pacific (Page) and Nigerian placenames and surnames in Japan (Baiye).

This shows a direct spread of Nigerian place names from Africa, across the Indian Ocean into the Pacific. The discovery of common placenames in three different regions can not be accounted by coincidence.These names had to have been carried by humans.

These people share similar placenames because when they left Nubia to settle West Africa and the Islands they named settlements after places in Nubia and the Saharan highlands.

CHAPTER 13: BLACKS IN SOUTHEAST ASIA

The Blacks of Southeast Asia and southern China were called Man, by the Chinese . This became the general Chinese term for African and Asiatic Blacks along with the term Kunlun. Up to the Tang Dynasty the south sea area was called **Kunlun**. The Chinese documents speak of Kunlun slaves, Kunlun people , Kunlun languages and Kunlun ships. Triptaka, a Chinese traveller to southern China and Southeast Asia observed that "the Cambodians remind me of the Man, our southern Chinese barbarians;they are coarse-featured and very dark".

GEOGRAPHY

Southeast Asia is characterized by long rivers. These rivers extend from Himalayan mountains down to the Indian Ocean.

The rivers which rise in the Himalayan mountains receive gigantic amounts of rain water during the summer monsoons. The monsoons are seasonal winds of the Indian Ocean which take

place twice a year:the southwest monsoon from June-September,
and the northwest monsoon from November -April.

Moisture from the Indian Ocean is carried by wind/ monsoon
to Southeast Asia. This moisture later becomes rainfall in this
region.

Nearness to the Equator, makes the climate hot in the region.
The vegetation in this area is tropical rain forest.

MAINLAND SOUTHEAST ASIA

Southeast Asia is divided into both a mainland and Island
region. The mainland is composed of numerous rivers including
the Irarawaddy and Salween in the West, and the Mekong river in
the East. The Irrawaddy and Salween rivers are situated in
Burma. The Mekong river flows through Laos, Kampuchea ,
Vietnam and South China.

There are three southern Asian countries situated on the
Malay Peninsula : Burma, Malaysia and Thailand. At the tip of this
peninsula we find Singapore. The vegetation in this area is
tropical year round.

Numerous mountains are found in mainland southeast Asia. The dense rainforest makes overland travel difficult. As a result people use rivers to move goods and themselves from place to place. Rivers are therefore the main transportation routes.

Island Southeast Asia

Island Southeast Asia includes the East Indies and Philippine Islands. The East Indies include the Islands of Sumatra, Java, Indonesia, Borneo, Celebs and New Guinea.

The Islands consist of a mountainous core, surrounded by coastal lowlands. The soil of these Islands due to volcanic ash is very rich. The cover of these Islands is tropical rain forest.

The Philippines are much further away from the the equator than the other Southeast Asian islands. The climate of these islands is much cooler than the other islands in the area.

ARCHAEOLOGY

Beginning around 10,000 BC, man began to make pottery. By 4,000 BC Blacks in Southeast Asia at a place called Non Nok Tha exploited plants and animals for food. They made fine pottery and raised rice. By 13,000 BC they had begun to grow crops and had domesticated several animals.

During the pleistocene period Southeast Asia was twice the size it is now. At this time Western Indonesia and the Philippines were connected to the mainland. Much of the original land mass was submerged when the continental glaciers melted and the sea began to raise. The people of south-east Asia lived peacefully as late as 2000 BC.

Around 10,000 BC various types of Blacks were living in Southeast Asia and South China. The Mongoloid people lived in the far North up until 3000 BC.

The Neolithic cultures of south China and Southeast Asia are related in characteristics of everyday life such as farming, the use of pottery and the making of stone instruments. In southern China the most well known early culture was Dapenkeng which dates to 5000 BC.

These Dapenkeng sites are best known for the appearance of cordmarked pottery. The color of the pottery ranges from buff to dark brown. The principal shapes of the vessels are large globular jars and bowls. The people of this culture also made many stone sinkers and the dugout canoe.

In addition to fishing for food these people grew root crops. These Blacks were spread from IndoChina to Southern China and Japan. The Hoabinhian and Dapenkeng cultures are characterized by the same type of pottery. The people in these cultures lived on top of mounds and piled houses.

In Hubeh (Hupeh) and Guangxi (Kwangsi), these ancient Asian Blacks cultivated their crops by artificial irrigation and by terracing of the mountain slopes. These technique were later taught to the Mongoloids by the Blacks. By 4500 BC these culture groups were using bronze to cast works of art.

The late neolithic technology inventories of China and Southeast Asia included the bow and arrow for hunting. Their pottery was painted and they made stone knives and sickles. Some of the pottery had three lands, just like their bronze work.

The people who formerly lived in Southeast Asia, spoke

Dravidian, Manding , Puntite and Austronesian languages. Today

some people speak Dravidian languages, but most people speak

Austro-Asiatic languages, which are closely related to the

Austronesian group. Dr. Shun-sheng Ling, believes that because

the aborigines of Hainan and Taiwan (Formosa) speak

Austronesian languages most of the earliest inhabitants of

Southeast Asia and South China probably spoke Austronesian.

Many Austronesians are considered part of the Africoid

population/race.

ORIGIN SOUTHEAST ASIAN PEOPLE

The archaeological evidence appears to indicate that

civilization in Southeast Asia came from South China. The

founders of civilization in this area were non-Mongoloid people:

Indo-African groups. Moreover, the Thai and Chinese speaking

groups did not enter Southeast Asia until after 500 BC.

Before 500 BC, the Kushana or Yueh people monopolized civilization in Southeast Asia. Around 3000 BC Negritos and Austroloid people were the masters of the Orient. The Australian/Austroloid people had crossed from Southeast Asia along a land bridge into Australia. The examples of this group include the Senoi of Malaya and the Vedda of Sri Lanka (Ceylon).

By 12,000 BC the land bridge to Australia was submerged under the Indian Ocean. Between 6000-3000 BC African-Dravidian type people began to occupy much of Asia. These folk later became the Melenesian people of China and Southeast Asia.

These Afro-Indian (Dravidian people) were called Yueh in the Chinese literature or Kushana. The Kushana people originally migrated from middle Africa to Iran. From Iran they migrated into Central Asia China and Yunnan.

The Kushana participated in the Lungshanoid neolithic culture which had wheeled vehicles, a system of writing and bronze working . The Kushana founded the Shang and Xia Dynasties. As early as 2000 BC the Yueh had cultivated Rice.

Professor Kwang Chih Chang, has suggested that people influenced by the Lungshan civilization began culture in much of Thailand. He believes that Lungshan culture reached the Mekong headwaters and spread throughout South-east Asia. Other Lungshan sites are near the Red River. It would appear that Kushana people living in Yunnan traveled down the Mekong and Red Rivers to establish civilization in Southeast Asia.

The Yueh/Kushana/ Kushite people may have founded culture at Phung Nguyen, and settled Ban Chiang after 2500 BC. At Phung Nguyen, settlers cultivated rice, practiced animal husbandry, and worked stone between 2500-1800 BC.

The Yueh also settled Ban Na Di, which dates to 1400 BC. The Yueh people spoke Dravidian and Manding languages.

From 500 BC up until the Christian era we find sudden changes in the pottery this suggest the arrival of an alien population. There are two types of Indonesians in Southeast Asia. The first type of Indonesian represents the tribal peoples such as the groups in the highlands of IndoChina and the Dayaks of Bornea . The second type of Indonesian has strong Mongoloid affinity related through typology to Japanese, e.g., the Cham, Malay and Javanese. The Thai and Vietnamese are the most marked Mongol types.

There is also one other group of the Southeast Asians. This is the Mon-Khmer group. The Mon-Khmer people found in Southeast Asia and India may be a mixture of Mongol and Proto-Melenesian elements.

The Yueh were a dominant power in Asia for several thousand years. Between 500 BC and A.D. 1000.

There were also Puntite speakers in Southeast Asia. These Puntite speakers came from Ethiopia. They were probably related to the people who founded the Arwe and Habesha-Axum empires. These Puntites, are usually referred too as the Naga or "Sea Kings.

SOUTH CHINA ROOTS

The founders of Southeast Asian civilization from Southern China were members of the Yueh tribe. These Proto-Tamil and

Manding speaking peoples moved from Yunnan into Southeast Asia.

The Yueh tribes began their civilization on the Yangtze and Mekong rivers . In Yunnan they had terraced fields, irrigation ditches, potter's wheels and both bronze and iron. In Yunnan the Yueh people built fortified settlements to protect their cities from the Hua (ancient name for modern Chinese group) and Thai tribesmen. The people in Yunnan grew millet, rice and wheat.

The decline of the Yunnan culture occurred in the southeastern part of the Province around the area of Lake Dien, not far from that part of north Vietnam were the Dongson culture originated. Here we find many Dongson bronzes at Shihzhaishan,Zhinningi and burials sites at Anning near Lake Dien.The usual symbol on the bronze weapons from these sites are serpents and birds resembling peacocks and cocks, the symbol of Siva worship. They had domesticated horses and Indian type cattle. The people wore traditional feathered plumes worn by the Kushana of Central Asia, and North India in Yunnan.

The Yueh people are the founders of the so-called "Hindu civilization of Southeast Asia. They are the Kosars, and Tamils of Indian literature and traditions. They are called Tamil, because the earliest group of Yueh or Kushanas to enter India came by way of Tamilitti, the great seaport at the mouth of the Ganges.

Also the symbols on Heger type drums from Yunnan, e.g., peacocks and headdresses are the same as Kushana artifacts of North India,who were also members of the Yueh tribe. Moreover the common style bronze kettle drums, bronze axes and weapons, cattle and peacock decorative motifs all point to a Kushana origin for these culture elements in Yunnan and later Southeast Asia.

Siva was a popular god among the Yueh people. The abode of Siva, was the snow capped mount Kailas, situated north of the Himalayas near the source of the Ganges river.

The Indo-Aryan literature of India, claims that Siva, gave the Deva people a long and hard struggle. The Tamilian form of Saivism is known as Agamas, the esoteric and ritualistic parts of Agama are called: Tantra. The Agama is non-Vedic (not of Indo-

European origin). Agama was also the Southeast Asian form of
Hinduism.

HISTORY

The Manding and Dravidian speaking people that made up the
Kushana group entered Southeast Asia from the south of China.
Another group of Africans entered southeast Asia by Sea.

The earliest group to influence Southeast Asia were the
megalithic people. These people have left megalithic sites,

Borneo - 700 A.D.

urns, dolmens and menhirs from southern Arabia through south

India on into Vietnam, Siam and Laos. By 500 BC this culture was

typified by a highly developed burial cult. Evidence of this culture include large burial urns carved from white sandstone found at these sites.

Under pressure from the Chinese many Proto-Melenesian Blacks left the area for the Islands. These Proto-Melenesian blacks spoke a language that combined many elements of Black African and Dravidian tongues.

The first group of seaborne settlers of Southeast Asia were the Naga of ancient Arwe and the Habesha-Axum empires .

FOU NAN AND KHMER

The Khmer kingdom, Fou Nan and Cochin China were once ruled by Blacks. As in India the culture bearers of Fou Nan were mainly Naga, a representative of local native royalty of Fou Nan. The Naga himself was an engineer.

Funan

Tradition has it that the Naga, drank the floodwaters and enabled the people to cultivate the fields. This tradition refers to the numerous ancient canals in Fou Nan designed to control the Mekong Delta floods, while irrigating large rice paddies without endangering the crops which were probably developed by the Naga himself.

The chief sites of Fou Nan, Oc-eo and Nai Sam, all had Dravidian style houses and buildings built on piles. The people here as in the Kushana areas of Central Asia and Qiang, wrote in Sanskrit. The Naga, who early ruled Cambay, may have been responsible for the spread of Dravidian carnelian beads to Southeast Asia as early as 1000 BC.

This Naga brings to mind the the Kings of Arwe called Nagast. The tax collector was called Nagashi. This similarity between the Naga of Fou Nan, and the Nagast of Arwe, is so striking that it suggest the possibility the Arwe and/or Axumite colonist may have been early established along the waterways of Southeast Asia. The cities of Fou Nan were laid out along the canals with boats used for transportation. The houses of Fou Nan were built on piles, and were reported to be very splendid.

The greatest IndoChinese civilization was Khmer Blacks who ruled over Ankor Wat for 600 years. The Khmer received much from the Hindus especially the Hinduized (Dravidian) Kings of Java who helped them exploit the fertile soil of the Mekong.

The Khmers were mainly Austro-Asiatic speakers. They practiced Human sacrifice and a form of spirit worship as in Ethiopia. Their houses were built on wooded stilts and thatched with leaves. They were already agriculturalists, and their is evidence they worked with metals.

Cambodia - (pre-Angkor)

Due to Dravidian influences the Khmers began to develop
their material culture. Their bronze work was superior to any
work done in the rest of IndoChina and they made beautiful
carvings in bricks. they were highly literate and honored their
poets.

The architecture of Ankor Wat, and other Khmer centers was typified by a series of compressed stories that formed the tower of each shrine, composing a series of several architraves, which take on the outline of a sprouting shoot. The second major characteristic of Khmer architecture are luxuriant, extremely fine foliate scroll relief carvings. In association with the great monuments are magnificent sculptures.

Many people think of the ancient Khmer as warriors, but they were mainly farmers. They used irrigation to grow rice. Dikes were used to move water along the canals or keep water in the reservoir to make sure it was available when needed.

The women of Khmer held high status in Khmer society. Many women such as Indradevi and Tikala, were acknowledged fine scholars.

Mon - 800 A.D.

213

The Khmers were very dark people with burnished skin nearly black. The hair was kinky, the same as that of Dravidians, Elamites and Minoans.

The Khmer civilization was destroyed by advancing Chinese races mainly Thais, while the Fou Nan culture was destroyed by the Annamites or Vietnamese. Most of these groups still show affinities to Africoid populations today.

DONGSON CULTURE

After being forced from Yunnan the Kushanas moved into the Mekong delta and founded the Dongson culture. This period is called the early metal age in Southeast Asia.

The Dongson culture of Tokin and Annam was the first IndoChina culture. Founded by the Kushana, this was a megalithic culture which extended from southern India into Southeast Asia. The people of Dongson made from 800-111 BC. They were defeated by the Mongoloid Chinese in 111 BC in the Tonkin area.

Dongson metallurgy and art spread into Thailand, Malaya, Indonesia and Java. The people worked iron and bronze. The common symbol for the Dongson Tamil speakers were birds, peacocks, deer and drums. The boats of the Dongson people had birdhead prows and tail feather sterns. These Dravidian people made dolmens. It was in IndoChina, that Dravidian and Manding speaking groups came in contact with the Puntite speaking Nagas.

Many researchers believe that the Dongson culture may have been the forerunner of the Melenesian cultures. Philip Rawson, in the Art of Southeast Asia, said it was the Dongson people that formed the base of the Melenesians.

The Tamils of Dongson culture also took Dongson culture to the Southeast Asian islands. The early metal period on the Islands dates from 500 BC to A.D. 1000, on Taiwan, the Philippines, Talaud,Serawaki, Java and Timor.

The metal age sites of the Sunda Islands od Dongson show affinity to western Melanesian styles. The Indonesian drums of the metal age, especially the Sangeang drum dating to A.D. 250

and friezes of elephants and peacocks from the Salayar Islands show a Kushana origin. The Sangeang drum of Indonesia depict men riding horses and wearing Kushana costumes.

Khmer, Cambodia

KAMBOJA

The empire of Khmer was called Kamboja. The original

Kamboja were not related to the present people that live in

Kampuchea. The Kamboja according to Bagchi, were members of

the Kushana tribes of Central Asia. From here

they migrated to the Mekong area and built Khmer along with the

Naga. It was the Kamboja Kushanas that later invaded Assam

and Bengal.

Champa King

CHAMPA

Another important empire in Southeast Asia was Champa.

Champa was ruled by Dravidians. Champa was later destroyed by

Vietnamese nomads as they expanded southward into present

day Vietnam.

Thailand 700 A.D.

THAI KINGDOMS

After the Thai tribes destroyed the chiefdoms of Khmer, the chieftains made an alliance in southern Siam and created the Kingdom of Lavo. After the Mongols took control of much of Kampuchea, the Thai formed the state of Siam, which we call Thailand today.

Both the Vietnamese tribes and the Thai tribes learned their culture , architecture, religion and writing from the Khmers.

Chapter 14 : African Origin of Dravidian Speaking People

There are two mtDNA and Y-Chromosome models used to

explain the origin of Dravidian speakers in India. One model

postulates a Pleistocene heritage for the Dravidian speakers

based on the diversity of hapalogroup M, in India[92] . Other

researchers have claimed a Middle East origin for the Dravidian

speaking people [93], eventhough Kivisild et al has confirmed that

there is a low-frequentcy of Eurasian mtDNA among Indians[94] .

Although these origin models are popular in the literature

there is another model for Dravidian origins that proposes that

Dravidians originated in Africa and migrated to India during the

[92] Barnabas, S.,Shouche, Y.,and Suresh,C.G. (2005). High resolution mtDNA studies of the Indian population: Implications for Paleolithic settlement of the Indian Subconinent, Annals of Human Genetics, 1-17; Thangaraj, Kumarasamy, Gyaneshwer Chaubey,Vijay Kumar Singh, Ayyasamy Vanniarajan, Ismail Thanseem, Alla G Reddy, and Lalji Singh. (2006). In situ origin of deep rooting lineages of mitochondrial Macrohaplogroup 'M' in India. BMC Genomics. 2006; 7: 151.
http://www.pubmedcentral.nih.gov/articlerender.fcgi? artid=1534032

[93] Quintana-Murci L, Semino O, Bandelt H-J, Passarino G, McElreavey K, Santachiara-Benerecetti AS. (1999) Genetic evidence of an early exit of Homo sapiens sapiens from Africa through eastern Africa.Nat Genet 1999, 23(4):437-441. [PubMed Abstract] [Publisher Full Text]

[94]Kivisild T, Bamshad MJ, Kaldma K, Metspalu M, Metspalu E, Reidla M, Laos S, Parik J, Watkins WS, Dixon ME, Papiha SS, Mastana SS, Mir MR, Ferak V, Villems R (1999). Deep common ancestry of Indian and western-Eurasian mitochondrial DNA lineages. Curr Biol 9:1331–1334

Neolithic. This model is supported by archaeological, linguistic and mtDNA and Y-chromosome data.

African and Indian Skeletal Data

Using craniometric data researchers have made it clear that the Dravidian speakers of South India and the Indus valley were primarily related to the ancient Caspian or Mediterranean population [95] . Lahovary and Sastri maintains that this population was unified over an extensive zone from Africa, across Eurasia into South India [96]. Some researchers maintain that the Caspian civilization originated in East Africa[97] .

Shared Archaeological Data

According to Sergent (1992), the Dravidian populations are not

---

[95] Winters, C.Did the Dravidians Originate in Africa. BioEssays , **2007,** 29(5) , 497 – 498, **and** Winters C. 2008. ARE DRAVIDIANS OF AFRICAN ORIGIN. International Journal of Human Genetics , http://www.krepublishers.com/02-Journals/IJHG/IJHG-08-0-000-000-2008-Web/IJHG-08-4-317-368-2008-Abst-PDF/IJHG-08-4-325-08-362-Winder-C/IJHG-08-4-325-08-362-Winder-C-Tt.pdf

[96] Winters, Did Dravidians Originate in Africa, passim ;and Sastri, Nulakanta. (1955). History of South India.Cumberledge, Madras .
[97]Cole, Sonia.(1954). The Prehistory of East Africa. London: Pelican.

autochthonous to India either, but of African origin. The

archaeological evidence also appears to support an African origin

for the Dravidian speaking people[98] .

Researchers have conclusively proven that the Dravidians are

related to the C-group of Nubia [99], given the fact that

both groups used 1) a common BRW[100] ; 2) a common burial

complex incorporating megaliths and circular rock enclosures and

3) a common type of rock cut sepulcher . The BRW industry

diffused from Nubia, across West Asia into Rajastan, and thence

to East Central and South India .

Singh made it clear that he believes that the BRW radiated

from Nubia through Mesopotamia and Iran southward into India.

BRW is found at the lowest levels of Harappa and Lothal dating to

---

[98] Lal BB. 1963. "The Only Asian Expedition in threatened Nubia: Work by an India Mission at Afyeh and Tumas". *The Illustrated Times,* London 20 April ; and Winters, Clyde Ahmad. (1985). The Proto-Culture of the⬚Dravidians,Manding and Sumerians, Tamil Civilization 3 (1), 1-9.

[99] Lal BB. 1963. "The Only Asian Expedition in threatened Nubia: Work by an India Mission at Afyeh and Tumas". *The Illustrated Times,* London 20 April
[100]Sastri, Nulakanta. (1955). History of South India.Cumberledge, Madras .

2400BC[101] . T.B. Nayar in <u>The problem of Dravidian Origins</u> proved that the BRW of Harappa has affinities to predynastic Egyptian and West Asian pottery dating to the same time period.

After 1700 BC, with the end of the Harappan civilization spread BRW southward into the Chalcolithic culture of Malwa and Central India down to Northern Deccan and eastward into the Gangetic Basin. The BRW of the Malwa culture occupied the Tapi Valley Pravara Godavari and the Bhima Valleys. In addition we find that the pottery used in Rajasthan on the banks of the Bana River, was also BRW.

Archaeologists agree that Black and red ware (BRW) was unearthed on many South India sites are related to Dravidian speaking people. The BRW style has been found on the lower levels of Madurai and Tirukkampuliyur.

Some researchers attempt to portray the Dravidians as Caucasoid people and try to link these people to western Eurasian people.

Other researchers in India attempt to postulate an Indian

---

[101] Singh, H.N. (1982). History and archaeology of Black-and Red ware. Delhi.

origin for Dravidians because they mainly belong to the M

haplogroup (HG).

Thangaraj et al recognize a Paleolithic origin of the M

HG. The majority of Dravidian speaking people belong to the M

haplogroup. Most geneticists agree that the M haplogroup is

derived from L3. Kivisild et al made it clear that all Indian mtDNA

lineages "coalesce finally to the African L3a".

Metspalu argues that the earliest offshoots for L3, were

HGs M and N developed in Arabia. Metspalu (2005) believes the

MRCA for the M HG entered Asia 60-65 kya.

Winters has shown that haplogroup M originated in Africa

before African out of Africa (AoA) exit 60kya[102]. Dr, Winters has

shown that haplogroup M had spread to the Senegambia region

before 60kya.

Metspalu maintains that "all the basal trunks of M, N

---

[102] Clyde Winters ,2011. The Demic Diffussion of the M-Haplogroup from East Africa to the Senegambia. BioResearch Bulletin ,4:51-54.

http://bioresonline.com/Documents/AA000168.pdf

and R have diversified in situ" [103] . He makes it clear that in

his opinion the M HGs are different from the subhaplogroup M of

East Asia . The most frequent HG in India is M2 .

Sixty percent of of the Indian mtDNA lineages are M HGs[104] .

Kivisild et al [105] , maintains that there are five M HGs in India:

M1, M2,M3, M4, and M5. Thanaraj et al , has revised the

classification of HGs M3, M18 and M31 and defined the novel HG

M41. Sun et al identified another 5 M haplogroups (M34-M40) in

addition to the Indian mtDNA macrohaplogroup N [106].

The diversity of M HGs in India has led many researchers to

suggest that the M clades have an in-situ origin .These

researchers speculate that although L3 originated in Africa, the

M1 HG in Ethiopia and Egypt ,may be the result of a back

migration to Africa from India.

These researchers base this theory for a back migration to

[103]Metspalu,M.(2005). Through the course of prehistory in India: Tracing the mtDNA Trail. Dissertation Biologicae Universitatis Tartnensis 114, {Tartu University Press) p.24.

[104]Thangaraj et al 2006, passim.
[105]Kivisild, Toomas, Katrin Kaldman, Mait Metspalu, Juri parik, Surinder Papiha.(1999b). In Genomic Diversity, (Ed.) R. Papiha Deka (pp.135-152). S.S. Kluwer/Plenum Publishers.
[106] Sun, Chang, Qing-Peng Kong, Malliya gounder Palanichamy,Suraksha Agrawal, Hans Jurgen Bandelt, Yong-Gang Yao, Faisal Khan, Chun-Ling Zhu, Tapas Kumar Chaudhuri, and Ya-Ping Zhang.(2005). Molecular Biology and Evolution,10, 1093.

Africa from India, on 1) HG M1 is not found in India; and 2) the M

HG's are only found in East Africa. Both of these theories have

little support when we look at the mtDNA data for Africa and

India.

Barnabas et al, noted that N,M and F lineages found in

India could have originated in Africa . He speculated

these people migrated to India from Africa during the Upper

Paleolithic.

Most researchers make it appear that the M1 haplogroup is

only found in Ethiopia. These researchers maintain that the M1

HG is restricted to the Afro-Asiatic linguistic phylum . This is false

M HGs are found in other parts of Africa where people speak non-

Afro-Asiatic languages.

The M lineages are not found only in East Africa. Rosa et al[107]

, found a low frequency of the M1 HG among West Africans who

speak the Niger Congo languages, such as the Balanta-Djola.

Gonzalez et al found N, M and M1 HGs among Niger-Congo

[107] Rosa, Alexandra, António Brehm, Toomas Kivisild1, Ene Metspalu and Richard Villems. (2004). MtDNA Profile of West Africa Guineans: Towards a Better Understanding of the Senegambia Region. Annals of Human Genetics, 68, 4 .
http://www.blackwell-synergy.com/links/doi/10.1046/j.1529-8817.2004.00100.x/enhancedabs/

speakers living in Cameroon, Senegambia and Guinea Bissau [108].

It is also not true that HG M1 is absent in India. Kivisild et al

found five M HGs in India: M1, M2, M3, M4 and M5 [109]. It is

interesting to note that the M4 HG has the same 16311 coding

region as the African M1 HG.

Kivisild et al, provides the first detailed discussion of

the M subclusters in India and suggested an autochthonous

development of these lineages in India[110]. The researchers

suggest that there were multiple M lineages when this haplogroup

migrated to Asia. These researchers claimed that the expansion

date for the five M subclusters expanded into India between

17,000-32,000 bp.

Kivisild et al noted that 26 of the subjects in his study

[108]González, A. M., V. M. Cabrera, J. M. Larruga, A. Tounkara, G. Noumsi, B. N. Thomas and J. M. Moulds. (2006). Mitochondrial DNA Variation in Mauritania and Mali and their Genetic Relationship to Other Western Africa Populations. Annals of Human Genetics 70,5. http://www.blackwell-synergy.com/doi/abs/10.1111/j.1469-1809.2006.00259.x?cookieSet=1&journalCode=ahg

[109] Kivisild, Toomas, Katrin Kaldman, Mait Metspalu, Juri parik, Surinder Papiha.(1999). In Genomic Diversity, (Ed.) R. Papiha Deka (pp.135-152). S.S. Kluwer/Plenum Publishers.http://evolutsioon.ut.ee/publications/Kivisild1999b.pdf

[110] Ibid, passim.

belonged to the M1 haplogroup [111]. It clear from this study that

sub-cluster M1 was found mainly in Kerala and Karnataka . An

interesting finding in the study was that most of the Indians with

the M1 HG were members of upper caste.

Haplotype Sharing between Populations

The H1 haplotype is found among many Dravidians. Sengupta

et al noted that the subclades H1 and H2 was found among 26%

of the Dravidian speakers in their study, especially in Tamil Nadu

[112]. Ramana et al (2001) claims that the discovery of H1 and H2

haplotypes among the Siddis is a "signature" of their African

ancestry. The frequency of the H1 subclade among Dravidian

speakers is also and indicator of an African-Dravidian connection.

In addition to haplotypes H1, in South India we also find

---

[111] Ibid., passim; and C. Winters2008a. Can parallel mutation and neutral genome selection explain Eastern African M1 consensus HVS-1 motifs in Indian M Haplogroups. Int J Hum Genet, 13(3): 93-96.
http://www.ijhg.com/article.asp?issn=0971-
6866;year=2007;volume=13;issue=3;spage=93;epage=96;aulast=Winters.
[112] Sengupta, Sanghamitra, Lev A. Zhivotovsky, Roy King, S. Q.
Mehdi,Christopher A. Edmonds, Cheryl-Emiliane T. Chow, Alice A. Lin,
Mitashree Mitra, Samir K. Sil, A. Ramesh, M. V. Usha Rani, Chitra M.
Thakur, L. Luca Cavalli-Sforza, Partha P. Majumder, and Peter A.
Underhill (2006)Am. J. Hum. Genet., 78:202-221.
http://www.journals.uchicago.edu/AJHG/journal/issues/v78n2/42812/42812.html?erFrom=321426987696
2983094Guest

the African 9-bp deletion [113]. Watkins et al found the 9bp motif among four Indian tribal populations: Irula, Yanadi, Siddi and Maria Gond.

The Dravidians were Kushites. The Kushites were predominately Niger-Congo speakers. The hundreds of words associated with this finding support a genetic relationship between Niger-Congo and Dravidian languages.Until you can show there is no evidence of a linguistic relationship you are living in a dream world [114].

In summary, Dravidian tribal populations and Africans also share several y-chromosome, HLA and mtDNA .

The 9bp transition at 16311 are congruent among Dravidians and West Africans . The analysis revealed that the Nadar and Fulani HLA indicate that the populations share a number of

[113] Clyde Winters (2010). 9bp and the Relationship Between African and Dravidian Speakers. Current Research Journal of Biological Sciences 2(4): 229-231. http://maxwellsci.com/print/crjbs/v2-229-231.pdf

[114] Clyde Winters (2007) Did the Dravidian Speakers Originate in Africa? BioEssays, 27(5): 497-498.

unique alleles including A*101, A*0211,A*03011, A*3303,

B*3501, B*3701, B*51011[115].

Shared y-chromosomes include H1, K2 or Y-DNA T-M70

(11%). The Highest frequency of T-M70 in the world is found

among the Fulani. In relation to y-chromosome H1, 22% of

Dravidians carry this haplogroup [116].

Sickle cell anemia is frequent among Africans and Dravidian

Tribal populations. It is interesting that the Arab-Indian and

Senegal haplotypes are both associated with a C!T mutation at

position -158[117].

[115] Clyde Winters (2012) Comparison of Fulani and Nadar HLA. Indian J Hum Genet [serial online] 2012 [cited 2012 Jul 1];18:137-8. Available from: http://www.ijhg.com/text.asp?2012/18/1/137/96686
[116] Clyde Winters (2010. **Y-Chromosome evidence of an African origin of Dravidian agriculture.** International Journal of Genetics and Molecular Biology, 2(3): 030 – 033. http://www.academicjournals.org/IJGMB/abstracts/abstracts/abstracts2010/Mar/Winters.htm

[117] Clyde Winters (2010) *Paper Advantageous Alleles, Parallel Adaptation, Geographic Location andSickle Cell Anemia among Africans Advances in Bioresearch,1(2):69-71.* http://www.soeagra.com/abr/vol2/12.pdf

The Dravidians belong to the M macrohaplogroup. Shared

Afro-Indo M haplogroups include M1, M30, and M33. The M1

haplogroup was especially evident among high caste people in

Kerela[118]

[118] Clyde Winters (2008) ARE DRAVIDIANS OF AFRICAN ORIGIN
http://www.krepublishers.com/02-Journals/IJHG/IJHG-08-0-000-000-2008-
Web/IJHG-08-4-317-368-2008-Abst-PDF/IJHG-08-4-325-08-362-Winder-C/IJHG-
08-4-325-08-362-Winder-C-Tt.pdf

Made in the USA
San Bernardino, CA
25 July 2013